101 QUESTIONS AND ANSWERS
ON THE BIBLE

I dedicate this with deep gratitude to so many people whose names, alas, I have never known or have escaped me, but whose faces and presence I recognize as they come back to lecture after lecture as I speak at different times and often in different places. This manifestation of their love of the Scriptures has been a resurgent source of encouragement for me. This book is their book, for their interest and question generated it.

101 QUESTIONS AND ANSWERS ON THE BIBLE

Raymond E. Brown, S.S.

PAULIST PRESS
New York/Mahwah, N.J.

Nihil Obstat
Rev. Myles M. Bourke, S.S.L., S.T.D.
Censor Deputatus

Imprimatur:
Rev. Msgr. Patrick J. Sheridan
Vicar-General, *Archdiocese of New York*

January 26, 1990

Library of Congress Cataloging-in-Publication Data

Brown, Raymond Edward.
    101 questions and answers on the Bible / by Raymond E. Brown.
        p.   cm.
    Includes index
    ISBN 0-8091-4251-1
    1. Bible—Examinations, questions, etc. I. Title. II. Title: Responses to one hundred
one questions on the Bible.
BS612.B77 1990
220—dc20   90-36022
                                                                       CIP

Published by Paulist Press
997 Macarthur Boulevard
Mahwah, New Jersey 07430

www.paulistpress.com

Printed and bound in the
United States of America

CONTENTS

INTRODUCTION

In the late 1950s I completed doctoral studies preparatory to teaching the Bible; and after a year when I received a fellowship to work on the unpublished Dead Sea Scrolls in Jerusalem, I returned to begin teaching biblical studies at St. Mary's Seminary in Baltimore. In 1960 I gave my first summer school on the Bible and in the intervening years, beyond my regular teaching, I suppose I have spoken a thousand times to groups of all sorts who were interested in hearing about the Scriptures. They have included assemblies of bishops, clergy of Catholic dioceses, clergy of churches other than my own, orders of sisters, and the many, many people who attend summer schools, institutes, congresses, and conferences. I have been struck over the years by how often, no matter what I lecture on, the questions that are posed in the period assigned for such questioning come back again and again to the same subjects. Of course, that repetition has been helpful to me, not only in gaining a sense of what people are interested in, but in shaping responses that I hope can better meet their needs. In their kindness, people have often told me that the question periods are just as meaningful as the lectures in deepening their appreciation of the Bible. And so I have decided to try to pull together some of my experiences in these question periods, the questions that I remember as the most asked, and to put in print responses to them.

Let me insist that these are the questions most asked *of me*. I suspect that a high percentage of them would be asked of any speaker on the Bible; yet inevitably, what I have written and what I have spoken on prompt some of the questions addressed. I have tried to shape the questions as I remember them. Some questions

1

are always asked with simply a sense of interest or curiosity. Other questions are asked with a slight defensiveness, because very frequently the topic of the question represents something that is a bit unsettling to the questioner. Sometimes, questioners are quite persistent. They have heard an answer, but it does not get to the exact point that they are after. These various tones I have tried to preserve. I debated with myself about the length of the responses in this book. Was it better to give very long responses to a few questions, or to have shorter responses that would produce further questions picking up points not treated fully in the first response? For the most part I decided on the latter course, since often that has been my experience in the question-and-answer periods after my lectures. People do not want another lecture in response to a question. They would rather have the chance to probe a response they have not found complete. Nevertheless some questions are complicated; and under actual circumstances from the podium (duplicated in this book) they require more detailed responses. Thus the readers will soon see the varied length of the responses to the 101 Questions.

I have tried to keep the level of the language in this book less formal and more conversational—not always successfully, I am sure. Sometimes the way people phrase their questions has stuck in my memory, even if I am unhappy with that phrasing. In those cases I have chosen in my response to point out why I do not like the way in which the question was cast, for that difference in wording often constitutes part of the issue that is being raised. By trying to keep reasonably faithful to the way I remember people casting a certain question, I am also paying tribute to the fact that awkward phrasing has at times kept me honest. Scholars generally prefer blander and less abrasive ways of treating a subject. For example, I would always deal with the issue of Peter in the New Testament by discussing various roles that he or his image played. Inevitably, after I do that, someone will press the point with the blunt, "bottom-line" question: Was he pope? I will not even have mentioned that term, but questioners will want the issue translated into a language they can evaluate. How one answers honestly and directly such awkwardly-phrased questions, without getting trapped in anachronisms, is part of the art of good responses.

Within question-and-answer periods, in my experience, one question on a topic has often led to others and produced a sequence that developed an issue. I decided to capitalize on that in this book; and so instead of putting *101 Questions* in haphazard order, or in the order of frequency or importance, I arranged them topically (see Analytic Table of Contents). Of course, I do not pretend that in any single question-and-answer period I ever got the complete sequence of questions that I have now placed under one topic, but often I got many of them. Moreover, in the phrasing of the questions themselves, I have reflected some of the strange sequences that I remember. For instance, the frequent question as to whether I believe there is a devil virtually never comes "out of the blue"; it almost always follows a discussion of the miracles of Jesus and his driving out demons. The even more frequent question about the existence of angels comes to me, not out of the treatment of some Old Testament passage, but after I have discussed the annunciation narrative where angels speak to Mary and Joseph. These experiences determine where I have placed the treatments of the demonic and the angelic. In other words, this book while arranged topically, is not purely systematic; the topical sequence reflects the patterns of thought that cause people to raise questions.

The choice of questions has *not* been dictated by my judgment of what constitutes the most important issues in biblical study. Rather the choice has been guided by the concerns of questioners who have addressed me on the podium over the years. I want to alert readers that this is a people's book, not primarily a scholar's book. For instance, I find of major importance for understanding the Early Church the little scene in Acts 6:1–6, the first dispute within the Christian church reported by that book, involving the Hebrews and the Hellenists. Yet unless I have delivered a lecture on that particular topic in Acts, people will never stand up in a general question period and start asking me about the Hellenists. On the other hand, no matter what aspect a lecture on the New Testament has concerned, someone may well get up and ask about the brothers of Jesus. The issue of whether the brothers of Jesus were the children of Mary is scarcely a major topic in the study of the New Testament, but it is a Bible-related issue that many meet in their own lives and is one of the things that has puzzled them.

That the questions in this book come from real questioners is responsible for the appearance not only of subjects that scholars might deem unimportant but also of subjects that scholars might prefer to avoid. I smile when people of wisdom suggest that a delicate topic like the virginal conception might better be avoided in public discussion, for it disturbs people (even though widely read news magazines and women's journals have spread sensationalist liberal views about it to a mass audience). Such delicacy is not a luxury one can enjoy on a lecture platform, for questioners have an instinct for unpleasantly difficult and sensitive issues. I remarked above that the blunt way in which questions are put may not allow the speaker easily "to get off the hook." Similarly the speaker learns that there is no unthinkable question. Someone out there will soon have thought of it.

Since I am a Roman Catholic priest and percentage-wise there have been more Catholics in audiences I address than Protestants or Jews, inevitably there will be a Catholic tone to many of the questions in this volume. Nevertheless, the fact that I have taught in a largely Protestant seminary for many years has alerted me to the fact that many issues, although phrased in a Catholic way, are of concern to others precisely because in their lives they are in contact with Catholics. I mentioned above the question of whether Mary had other children or remained a virgin. That question is often posed to me by Protestants because they want to see how a Catholic who claims to be a biblical scholar can hold a view of Mary that they regard as so unbiblical. In response to the questions in this volume I trust that it will be clear that I am one who accepts the doctrines of his church; yet I trust that it will be equally evident that I have tried to lay out the biblical evidence as objectively as possible and to make clear where the biblical evidence stops and where the interpretation of the Bible within the life of the church over the centuries adds new insights. If the biblical evidence is in itself ambiguous, in my judgment all should know that. I see no reason why Christians of diverse churches cannot agree on what the biblical evidence is and what the authors who wrote the Scriptures meant (to the degree that that is discernible by scholarship). Inevitably, they will disagree on what meaning the Bible has in various aspects of the life of the church, but the focus of the disagreement is then clearer. Most often, they will be arguing about something that is not clear in the Scriptures, but where diverse stances have been taken in the course of time. That helps to remove from inner-Christian debates the charge that one side is unbiblical; most often the same biblical evidence is being interpreted in different ways, and both sides in their lights are being loyal to the Bible.

Others who have spent their lives studying the Bible might well answer these questions in a different way. My replies are my own, but are shaped by a desire to make a position understood rather than eye-catching. I have found that an overly clever rejoinder or a repartee that aims at drawing laughs often offends and closes the mind of the questioner to what one is really trying to convey. I would rather ploddingly spell out what I think than expose to ridicule another type of answer, no matter how ridiculous I really think it is. I forewarn the readers that there will be little that is scintillating in the responses; I shall be satisfied if they find enough that is informative. I have chosen the word "Response" rather than answer to designate my reply to questions. This is how I have and would respond to questions, but the readers will have to decide whether they think the question has truly been answered.

ANALYTIC TABLE OF CONTENTS

(indicating the topics treated by the questions and responses)

THE 101 QUESTIONS AND RESPONSES

Q. 1. What is the best Bible to read?

The most appropriate Bible translation must be judged from one's purpose in reading. Public reading, as on Sunday or in other communal services, requires a certain solemnity; therefore, highly colloquial translations are not appropriate for that purpose. Private reading, on the other hand, for the purpose of spiritual reflection and refreshment, is sometimes best served by a translation that has an eye-catching, "user friendly" style. Other private reading is for the purpose of careful study; and then a more literal translation that preserves the difficulties and ambiguities of the original would be more desirable.

Perhaps the best overall answer I can give you is to point out that in the original Hebrew, Aramaic, and Greek texts of the biblical books, there are phrases that are difficult to understand or are ambiguous. Sometimes the authors did not write clearly. Translators have to guess at meaning a certain percentage of the time. Therefore, they must make a choice either to translate literally and preserve the obscurity of the original, or to translate freely and resolve the ambiguity of the original. A literal translation needs to be accompanied by footnotes or commentary suggesting possible resolutions of the obscurity that has been preserved in the translation. A free translation represents a choice already made by the translators as to what *they* think an obscure passage means. In a sense the commentary is built into the translated text. For that reason a free translation is easier to read but harder to make the subject of careful study.

Q. 2. Which translation do you recommend?

Among the literal translations (and I work with those more because I teach and want students to be aware of the problems in the text), there are four or five that can be used with profit. I should caution you that in the late 1980s and early 1990s almost all the major translations are undergoing major revision, and one needs to be careful when buying a Bible to obtain the latest form of the particular edition.

The Bible I use most is *The Revised Standard Version.* While it has difficulties (it is a revision of the *King James Version* and, unfortunately, at times, stays too close to the occasional bad instincts in the *King James*), it is for the most part both readable and carefully literal. One annoying factor for Catholics may be the use of archaic "Thou" and "Thee" in speaking to God; but that is being changed in the *New Revised Standard Version* of 1990. By far this is the Bible mainline Protestants use most, although often conservative Protestants still prefer the *King James.*

Probably Catholics in the U.S.A. use most *The New American Bible;* almost always that is what is read from the pulpit on Sunday. The Old Testament of that translation is excellent and for the most part better than *The Revised Standard Version.* The original New Testament part of the *New American* translation, however, was seriously defective, in part (especially for the Gospels) because it had been heavily rephrased after it left the hands of the original translators. Some bad choices were made, e.g., to render "the kingdom of God" by "the reign of God." (Besides the problem of the accuracy of such a rendition, which clearly does not fit some Gospel passages that describe a place [kingdom] rather than an action [ruling], there is the factor of comprehension. Parish audiences may often hear "rain" instead of "reign," since the latter is a rarely used term.) However, now this issue is no longer relevant, since the New Testament in *The New American Bible* was totally redone in the late 1980s, and is due to be introduced in the liturgy in the early 1990s.

British Catholics use *The Jerusalem Bible* in the liturgy, and this translation has had ecumenical appeal. In its first English edition the translation had many defects, since the English had largely been rendered from the French, sometimes without sufficient attempt to go back to the original languages. (The French was a more accurate translation.) Again, however, that judgment is now out of date in the light of a solid revision done in the 1980s. The informative footnotes of *The Jerusalem Bible* were very valuable and indeed have been improved in *The New Jerusalem Bible.*

Q. 3. What about popular translations? Are there any you do not like?

I have enjoyed reading many of the freer translations, especially when those who made them were adept in the choices that removed the obscurity of the original. As I have insisted, a free translation has, in a sense, a commentary built in to the translation. When I was in seminary the "Chicago Bible," with the New Testament done by E. J. Goodspeed, was very popular; and it remains a very useful Bible for personal reading. "Today's English Version" —*The Good News Bible*—is still very popular today and a highly intelligible version.

There is one free translation that I do *not* recommend: "The Living Bible." It is professedly a paraphrase: "A restatement of the author's thought, using different words than he did." I do not mind the paraphrase; but I do mind the rigid ultraconservative evangelical tone that at times, in my judgment, produces mistranslations. One can detect problems of this translation and test it by reading the beginning of John's Gospel. In the first verse it has "In the beginning was Christ." The original Greek is literally translated "In the beginning was the Word." Since "Christ" is a designation for the Word Incarnate, I deem it theologically inaccurate to say "In the beginning was Christ." "Christ" came to be when the Word became flesh. Such a paraphrase goes beyond translation to injudicious substitution.

Q. 4. Some of the Bibles you have been talking about are Protestant Bibles. Aren't Catholics forbidden to read Protestant Bibles?

One has to distinguish between the earlier Catholic position and the more recent position. The Bible was a subject of great debate between the Reformers and the theologians of the Council of Trent. In the Catholic judgment, the vernacular translations, that is the translations into the various national languages done by the Reformers, were often slanted to favor Protestant positions. Consequently, the Council of Trent insisted that in public reading, sermons, and explanations, the Latin Vulgate Bible used in the church for so many centuries should continue to be employed. The practical effect of this was that Catholic translations of the Bible were based on the Latin Vulgate, whereas Protestant translations of the Bible were done from the original languages (Hebrew, Aramaic, and Greek).

Moreover, the Catholic Church wanted the footnotes to respect both its teachings with regard to faith and morals and the interpretations of the Church Fathers. (A Protestant translation of the 1500s, the *Geneva Bible,* had clearly anti-Catholic notes, but the *King James Version* was not accompanied by footnotes.) Accordingly Catholics were instructed not to read Protestant Bibles lest they be subtly indoctrinated against their own faith. On the other side, certainly Protestants did not read Catholic Bibles, in part because of the supposition that these Bibles were inaccurate and contained church teaching in disguise.

All of this has changed. Beginning in the 1950s, Catholic translations, even those used in public reading and sermons, have been from the original languages. For instance, that is true of *The New American Bible* and *The New Jerusalem Bible* mentioned in the previous question. *The Revised Standard Version* has appeared in the Oxford Annotated Bible edition with footnotes of an informative and nonprejudicial nature, even as most of the footnotes in *The New Jerusalem Bible* are informative. While there may remain polemicists on both sides, the Bible is no longer a weapon of warfare between the mainline Protestant churches and the Roman Catholic Church. Catholics have had a part in the latest revision of *The Revised Standard Version* and Protestants shared in the latest revision of *The New American Bible.* We are helping each other to understand the Bible now. The Catholic reader can enjoy *The Revised Standard Version* or *The New English Bible* (or their recent revisions) without doctrinal apprehension.

Q. 5. But don't Catholics and Protestants have a different Bible in the sense of contents?

So far as the New Testament is concerned both Catholic and Protestant Bibles have the same number of books (27) in the same order. (That was not true of the early editions of Luther's translation of the New Testament, so far as order is concerned; but Luther's change of the order of the books is a footnote of history.) The difference lies in the Old Testament. To oversimplify, Jews and most Protestants have a Testament containing 39 books, while the Catholic Old Testament contains 46 books. I say "oversimplify" because the Church of England or Episcopal Church position is not unanimous (and one could debate whether the Anglican Church should be classified in the Protestant camp). Indeed many Protestant churches have never committed themselves officially to the number of Old Testament books. Another ambiguity is that the Orthodox and Eastern Churches at times have agreed with the longer canon that Catholics use or have proposed an even larger canon.

But if we simplify and talk about the Protestant and Catholic position, the seven books that are in the Catholic Old Testament and lacking in the Protestant Old Testament are called by Catholics deuterocanonical books—admittedly a mouthful. They are often called by Protestants the Apocrypha. They consist of Tobit, Judith, 1–2 Maccabees, Wisdom (of Solomon), Sirach (Ecclesiasticus), and Baruch (including the Epistle of Jeremiah); and for good measure one should throw in parts of Esther and Daniel. The issue is quite complex, but overall one may say that these are books that were preserved *in Greek,* not in Hebrew or Aramaic. (Some of them were originally written in Hebrew or Aramaic—large parts of the Hebrew Sirach have now been discovered—but not preserved in those languages.) They became known to Christians through the Septuagint, that is, the Greek translation made by Jews before Christ which became the commonly accepted Bible of the Early Church.

In their desire to translate from the original languages, the Reformers grew very suspicious of these books which were not available in Hebrew or Aramaic and for the most part rejected them. The issue was further complicated because Catholic theologians resorted to these books for support for doctrines that the Reformers rejected. For instance, the prayer of Judas Maccabeus and his men in 2 Macc 12:42–46 that the sinful deeds of the deceased soldiers might be blotted out in light of the resurrection of the dead was interpreted as support for purgatory. One Reformation response was to discredit that book as Scripture.

Q. 6. Will there ever be agreement on the Old Testament books that the Protestants do not accept?

I cannot conceive that in the foreseeable future there will be an official statement by a Protestant church body that it now accepts the seven disputed Old Testament books as canonical Scripture. Most Protestant churches would find it difficult to agree on an authority that could make such a statement. Since the Roman Catholic Church has officially committed itself at the Council of Trent to these books as Scripture, there is no chance that there will be a change in the Catholic position.

But having presented the bad news, let me turn to the good news. As with many sharp controversies of the 16th century, we are often finding a way around head-on confrontation—an "end run," if one may use football parlance. Many Bibles that are produced under Protestant auspices now contain the seven books (plus the parts of Esther and Daniel) under the name Apocrypha; for instance both *The Revised Standard Version* and *The New English Bible* are published in "Complete Bible" forms containing these books. Generally, they are not mixed in with the books that all consider canonical, as they are in Catholic Bibles, but published as a section either between the two Testaments (the better choice) or at the end, after the New Testament.

This inclusiveness is not a statement that they are canonical Scripture but a recognition of two ecumenical facts. The first is that Catholics now read Protestant Bibles and want what they consider a complete Bible. The second is that Catholics and Protestants study the Bible together, and these books are extremely important for the understanding of early Judaism (the Judaism that began after the exile in Babylon in 587–539 B.C.) and for the New Testament. They were written much closer to Jesus' time than many books of the universally accepted Old Testament, and they contain instances of ideas and outlooks that he accepted. (For instance, both the Books of the Maccabees and the Book of Wisdom testify to a belief in life after death.) Thus these books are necessary for the study of Scripture. As Protestant readers and students become familiar with the deuterocanonical writings, some of the old suspicions begin to disappear; and they are not looked on as hostile weapons in the hands of adversaries. By the way, it is interesting to note that next to the Psalms, Sirach (Ecclesiasticus) was the Old Testament book most used by the Church Fathers, for they found in it a mine of ethical teaching that could be of service for Christian instruction.

Q. 7. You said that Protestants and Catholics agree on the books of the New Testament. What about the apocryphal gospels that I hear about?

Your question helpfully reminds me that there are two senses in which the word "apocrypha" is used. It is used in Protestant parlance for the seven deuterocanonical books that I have just been discussing—the Old Testament books that Catholics accept as Scripture and Protestants do not. (Again I remind you that this is a shorthand identification.) But the term is used more widely of Jewish and Christian books that neither Catholics nor Protestants consider as Scripture. "Apocrypha" include Jewish books like *Enoch, Jubilees,* and *IV Ezra* that were not accepted in the commonly agreed on canonical Scriptures known to us, even though some of them were accepted in the Ethiopic Church. The term "Apocrypha" is also applied to Christian works, including gospels that were not accepted into the canon. Some of these have been preserved from antiquity. I think particularly of *The Protevangelium of James,* which is very important for understanding Christian attitudes toward the infancy of Jesus. (See Q. 10, 67, 68 below.) Some of the apocryphal gospels, although known in antiquity, have been lost and only rediscovered in modern times. A famous one is part of *The Gospel of Peter* which is an imaginative narrative of the passion. In particular, in the late 1940s, there was discovered in Egypt at Nag Hammadi or Chenoboskion a collection of (mostly gnostic) writings which were popularly, but inaccurately, touted as gnostic gospels. Among them there is an occasional gospel, the most famous of which is *The Gospel of Thomas.*

Q. 8. Is there a chance that any of the New Testament apocrypha will one day be recognized as genuine Scripture?

Here I must answer a question with questions. How does a church recognize works as Scripture? Is there an authority in the church to do this? On what principles? The very constitution of many Protestant churches would make impossible an authoritative statement recognizing new Scripture. The Roman Catholic Church has an acknowledged authority that could take such an action, but the Catholic principle for recognizing Scripture would forbid it. At the Council of Trent the guiding principle for acknowledging canonical Scripture was the long and universal use of books in the church for public reading. Therefore, even if a lost ancient book is discovered, for instance a letter genuinely written by Paul, the very fact that such a book has not been read in the church should mean that it would not be accepted as canonical. If we understand Scripture as the collection of books to the authority of which the church has agreed to bind itself because it has recognized in them God's inspired word, then a newly found book never previously used does not fit the criterion.

Q. 9. How valuable are the apocryphal gospels?

Sometimes scholars who are involved in either the discovery of hitherto lost works or the publication of them are not above sensational announcements; and, of course, even without their cooperation the press enjoys sensationalizing. If I may generalize, with a hint of cynicism, readers who have no interest in working through the canonical Gospels to learn about Jesus seem to be entranced by any new work that might hint that Jesus came down from the cross, married Mary Magdalene, and went off to live happily in India!

Let me give you a series of *my* judgments on recently discovered apocryphal gospels. (They are firm judgments and I suspect some will regard them as narrow, but I think they can be defended.) No recently discovered apocryphal gospel tells us a single biographical, historical fact about the life of Jesus that we have not known previously. Occasionally, a recently discovered gospel (especially the *Gospel of Thomas*) may give us a form of a saying of Jesus earlier than the form preserved in the canonical Gospels. Very rarely a recently discovered gospel may give us an authentic saying of Jesus that was not preserved in the canonical Gospels. The idea that recently discovered gospels tell us what the *earliest* Christians (A.D. 30–70) were like or thought, and that by contrast the canonical Gospels represent a highly censored and patriarchal version of Christianity, suppressing the freedom of the earliest Christian movements, is a distortion. What the apocryphal gospels do tell us is how Christians of the second century (and even later) thought about Jesus, how they filled in *imaginatively* details of his life where the canonical Gospels had left lacunae, and how they made him the spokesman of their own theology. Some of these gospels do so in a manner that the Church Fathers regarded as orthodox; some do it in a manner that they regarded as heretical. Thus to answer your question about whether the recently discovered apocryphal gospels have value, I would say yes—they have value for helping us to understand the many-faceted Christian groups of the second and third and fourth centuries. They have practically no value for giving us historical information about Jesus or about Christianity before the deaths of Peter and Paul in the 60s.

Q. 10. I thought I had heard that some of the apocryphal gospels had major influence on Catholic thought. Is that true?

Perhaps you remember that when I first began responding about the New Testament apocrypha (Q. 7 above), I made a distinction between those known and copied from antiquity and the gnostic works recently discovered. In the first group I mentioned *The Protevangelium of James,* probably to be dated from the mid-second century, which was copied and used in the church through the centuries. That work had great influence on the Christian portrayal of Mary, for it tells imaginatively of her background before the annunciation by Gabriel. From it came the names of Mary's parents, Joachim and Anne. From it also came the story of Mary being presented at the Temple at an early age—a presentation that has become a feast of the Catholic Church and has been portrayed by countless artists in paintings found in the art galleries of the world. From it, too, has come the portrayal of Joseph as an elderly man carrying a lily, since his staff is said to have blossomed as a sign that he was the one to be awarded Mary's hand in marriage.

The presentation of Mary, by the way, provides a chance to think maturely about the value of such a popular apocryphal gospel. Surely a female child like Mary would not have been brought to the high priest to live in the Temple precincts till the age of puberty, as *The Protevangelium* portrays. Yet this is an imaginative, narrative way of emphasizing a truth already implied by Luke in the canonical Gospel. The angel Gabriel speaks to Mary (Luke 1:28, 30) as to one who has already been "favored" by God (past tense); Mary speaks of herself as the handmaid (servant) of the Lord (1:38, 48). While the conception of God's Son at the annunciation was the principal favor or grace given by God to Mary, it came to one who had already been the subject of God's favor. Why? Because she had already subjected herself to God as His servant or handmaid. The annunciation was not the first time in Mary's life that she had said, at least in her heart, "Behold the handmaid of the Lord; be it done to me according to your word" (Luke 1:38). *The Protevangelium* has dramatized this by showing Mary presented and dedicated to God from her earliest youth. That dramatization would be understood on a popular level far more effectively than could a theological discussion of the implication to be derived from the past tense of the Greek verb for "favored."

Q. 11. Let's come back to the Bible we all accept. For people who are starting to read the Bible seriously, how do you recommend that they read it? Should they start with Genesis and read right through

to the Book of Revelation? Or should they select certain books at first?

Your question touches on a real problem, and I am not sure that there is a universal answer. In part the answer may depend on the temperament, background, and abilities of the readers. There are many stories about enthusiastic people who set out to read the Bible and got bogged down in genealogies or laws about sacrifice in the first five books and never made it to the other side.

Let us imagine your question applies to readers who have had high school and/or college educations, but have little knowledge of the Bible. (Unfortunately, it is still possible to get all the way through college and not to have had a really good introduction to the Bible.) In that case, it might be better to read biblical books that are by their very nature more attractive and intelligible than to work through every page of the Bible on the first attempt. *The Reader's Digest* has offered a shortened form of the Bible, designed to help readers who might bog down in the whole Bible.

I can imagine readers who might go profitably from Genesis to the first part of Exodus, then to parts of Judges, Samuel and Kings, getting a sense of story of the monarchy. They might then want to pick up the story at the end of Kings through parts of Ezra and Nehemiah to 1 Maccabees, in order to see what happened when the monarchy fell and the Jews returned from exile. Then sections from the Prophetic and Wisdom Books could give a sampling of the religious thought of Israel as expressed by its greatest spokesmen. The Psalms, those magnificent prayers stemming from different experiences of life, are intelligible and moving, even without the background of the story of Israel.

In the New Testament, readers might begin with the Gospels of Mark and John, turning next to the Book of Acts, sampling a few of the Pauline letters (e.g., 1 Corinthians and Philippians) as well as 1 Peter to get the spirit of the Early Church. With that sort of a quick passage through the less difficult portions of the Bible, one could be better prepared to undertake the reading of the whole. But I stress again that I am very uncertain about how this would appeal to

readers of different temperaments. Perhaps the best advice is to try
it and see what works best for yourselves.

Q. 12. What about notes or commentaries as a help?

That is a difficult question because there are such diversities
among Bible aids. In my judgment, it is always better to read a Bible
with footnotes that solve immediate difficulties arising from the
obscurity of the text or from the need for background.

When it comes to commentaries, one may distinguish at least
four types. There are fairly simple *pamphlet-style* commentaries.
Some of those have the text on one page or on the top of the page
and a brief commentary opposite or below. Perhaps a pamphlet of
75–100 pages covers a whole book of the Bible. These can be very
helpful and, indeed, adequate for most Bible readers. For those who
get into more serious study, there is the *paperback-book* length
commentary on an individual, major book of the Bible. These
commentaries will often run to 200 or 300 pages. For the most
serious student, of course, there is the *exhaustive verse-by-verse*
commentary that can run as long as 1500 pages on a book of the
Bible. I myself managed to write an 800-page commentary on the
relatively short letters of John; and I am not sure whether that is a
testimony to supposed erudition or to longwindedness. And then,
one should mention a long *single-volume* commentary on the
whole Bible. The most popular one among Roman Catholics has
been *The Jerome Biblical Commentary* or now *The New Jerome
Biblical Commentary,* published by Prentice Hall (eds. R. E.
Brown, J. A. Fitzmyer, R. E. Murphy); however, I would emphasize
that this one-volume commentary is really for more serious study.
The best start is the help provided by the pamphlet commentaries.

**Q. 13. But with notes and commentaries, are we not just getting
opinions about the Bible? Do we have to depend on scholars in order
to understand the Bible?**

Perhaps I could get at the root of your question by making
some observations. Often, those who have a desire to read the Bible

do not want to be told that only scholars have the key to the Bible and that unless they are willing to become scholars they cannot read the Bible. I agree fully with that reaction. There are sections of the Bible that are intelligible and spiritually nourishing without technical scholarly assistance. God can speak to the reader without the permission of scholars.

Nevertheless, when the readers about whom I was speaking—readers with a high school or college education—come to the Bible, they often start asking questions that spring from their education. They have learned a certain amount about science, and so they start wondering as they read Genesis whether the world really was created in six days, or was there not a long evolutionary process. Did the sun really stand still as described in Joshua 10:13?—a question provoked by the fact that such readers were taught that the sun does not revolve around the earth, but the earth revolves around the sun, and that the sun is moving within the total solar system. To answer questions that arise from one's general education, one needs a comparable education in how to read the Bible. One may not need the assistance of scholars to find spiritual nourishment; but one may need it to find answers to educated questions, even on a popular level.

Q. 14. I can see the need for some information supplied by scholars, but I don't see why we should be told that we are dependent on human interpretation of the word of God. Why such human intermediaries?

Every word in the Bible was written down by a human being, and so human attempts to understand the Bible are perfectly appropriate aids. The use of human intermediaries is, in my judgment, intrinsic to the Judeo-Christian conception of God's actions.

Part of the problem involved in this type of question may be the recognition that scholars change their mind, and therefore, there is an uncertainty about the opinions one finds in notes and commentaries. That is part of the human condition. What one needs to avoid, however, is the idea that older views were safe and modern views are changeable. Older interpretations of the Bible were scholarly opinions of previous centuries; modern views are scholarly opinions of this century—neither has a privileged or unchangeable status. The reader should be responsible only for seeking out the best scholarship available. If there are better ideas in the 21st century, or the 22nd, let the readers of that future period worry about them. And if you object, "Were my ancestors in Christianity misinformed when they read the Bible with the views of their time?", the answer is that presumably they did the best they could with the information then available and therefore fulfilled all their responsibilities. If we do as well with the information available to us, we can stand before the throne of God without guilt.

Q. 15. All of this sounds like private interpretation of the Bible. I thought Catholics gloried in not having to depend on private interpretation, but in having a church to tell them what the Bible means.

That is an oversimplified understanding. The Roman Catholic Church (and this would be true of the Eastern Churches as well) places a strong emphasis on the value of traditional faith attested through the ages. The reason for this emphasis is a belief that Christ through the Spirit continues to guide the church and will not allow it to err seriously in what it demands of its people by way of doctrinal and moral commitment. Therefore, when in the name of private interpretation of Scripture, someone stands up and says "What you have believed by way of doctrine for five centuries, or ten centuries, or twenty centuries is all wrong; you must give that up because here is how *I* interpret the Bible," the Catholic Church has resisted. The type of private interpretation that the Catholic Church distrusts involves doctrinal statements based on interpretations of the Bible that deny what has been taught in the creeds or in the official pronouncements of the church.

On the other hand, the Catholic Church has not issued official interpretations of Scripture as to the areas treated by most modern commentaries. Ordinarily, the commentator is seeking to discern what the original author of a biblical book sought to convey when he wrote a passage and what the people who read it in the author's time would have understood by it. The commentator is not normally attempting to establish doctrinal positions that would bind readers today. In terms of what we might call the literal sense of Scripture, i.e., what a verse meant when it was first written, it is doubtful that the Roman Catholic Church has ever defined the meaning of any passage. The church has defined that some of its doctrines are related to scriptural passages, but not necessarily that those doctrines were in the minds of the people who wrote the passages. Thus, a conflict between private interpretation and church doctrine based on Scripture is really not relevant to the type of commentary help that I have been describing.

I remember with sad amusement the observation made by a reviewer in a popular evaluation of a long commentary I had done. He stated that he was grateful that he did not have to bother with my opinions or those of others since he preached only what the Catholic Church taught about this particular book. Since the church had never interpreted the literal meaning of any passage in that book, I wondered exactly what he found to preach. What he really meant, I am sure, is that he preached the opinions about the book that he had been taught when he was in the seminary, and he did not want to bother seeing whether those opinions still represented where most scholars stood today.

Q. 16. Have you ever found a conflict about what the Catholic Church teaches based on Scripture and your interpretation of biblical texts?

No. And I say no not simply because, as I have reported above, the Catholic Church has not concerned itself in its doctrinal statements with the literal sense of Scripture (in the way I explained "literal"), but for deeper reasons. *First,* one must be very careful about what constitutes church doctrine. Often people consider everything they were taught in religion classes in grammar school to be church doctrine; yet at times that was an amalgamation of doctrine, opinion, and pious beliefs. The field of church doctrine is really rather narrow. I shall, I am sure, exemplify that in my responses to other questions that I will be asked.

Second, even where truly there is doctrine involved, often only with the help of scholarship has the church isolated what is doctrine from what has been simply a convenient way of expressing it. For instance, it is church doctrine that God created the world. For many centuries, those who proclaimed that may well have understood it to be part of the doctrine that God created the world exactly as described in the opening chapters of Genesis. Under the impact of modern scholarship about Genesis, the Catholic Church is now very clear that the doctrine of God's creating does not include the manner in which He created it. Therefore one is free to hold that the early chapters of Genesis are not a historical account of creation and to accept evolution.

Third, precisely because I recognize that sometimes what seemed very clear to the scholars of one century was judged wrong by the scholars of the next century, I do not have any supreme confidence in my own scholarship as if it were infallible. Because of the limited questions answered by scholarship and the careful self-confinement of the Catholic Church's doctrinal formulations, I really cannot see that there could be a conflict between what I uncover as the literal sense of the Scriptures and what the Catholic Church teaches as a doctrine based on Scripture. But were someone to point out a real conflict, my attitude would be similar to that which I have heard attributed to H. L. Mencken when he got angry letters from readers who disagreed with him. He had a printed card which said "Dear Sir or Madam, you may very well be right." Mencken's tone was sarcastic; mine is sincere: I may very well be wrong. However, when what the challengers are proposing is not really doctrine but their *interpretation* of doctrine, then I (or any other scholar) have the right to demand that scholarly reasons be brought forward to show who is right and who is wrong. In other words there is rarely an occasion of conflict between a biblical scholarship that respects the limitations of its own research and genuine church doctrine. No matter how the conflict is disguised, most often it is between two scholarly interpretations, one of which is posing as church doctrine. Fortunately, in my life, and in recent Roman Catholic Church experience in general, in the *biblical field,* there has been no tension between scholarship and official church teachers. That is not true of other fields of theological endeavor.

Q. 17. I thought there has been a lot of conflict between biblical scholars and official church teachers.

The answer depends on the tense of your verb: there had been conflict in the earlier part of this century. But from the time of Pope Pius XII in the 1940s and the Vatican Council II in the early 1960s, there has been remarkable harmony between biblical scholars and official church teachers. (Perhaps I should underline the word "official"; there are a small number of vocal ultraconservative Catholics who think that their interpretations of church doctrine are official and that they constitute a magisterium that can judge scholarship—this is a group I often call the third magisterium, consisting of self-appointed vigilantes who have no real status to speak for the church.) You can get a very good description of the conflict that existed before the Second Vatican Council, over a period of many years, in the work by Gerald P. Fogarty, *American Catholic Biblical Scholarship* (San Francisco: Harper & Row, 1989).

The single most important factor in changing the picture was the positive support given to modern biblical scholarship by Pope Pius XII, so that biblical scholars came to look upon the Pope and eventually upon Roman offices like the Pontifical Biblical Commission from the 1960s on as friends rather than as censorious opponents. In the last quarter-century there has been support in both directions and no hostility between biblical scholars and official church teachers. Personally, I have often expressed my indebtedness to the support I have received from the bishops of the Roman Catholic Church in the United States and, indeed, from several papal or Roman appointments that I have held. I do not interpret this as support for my individual views or a statement that I am always right, but as a recognition that Catholic scholars properly trained in modern biblical criticism are regarded as a positive contributing group in the larger church enterprise of proclaiming the Gospel.

Q. 18. What would you give as the most important reason for reading the Bible?

Perhaps I should distinguish a theological response and a practical response. Theologically, the clear response is that the Bible is

God's word in a unique way that is not true of any other human composition. Catholics have often been accused of giving the Bible a low level of appreciation; and yet the Second Vatican Council stated that the church is not above the word of God but serves it, and that we owe the word of God in the Scriptures a reverence similar to the reverence we have for the Word of God enfleshed in the eucharist.

That theological reasoning may seem a bit remote to many people, and I would like to offer a practical and personal reason that I have found most important in reading the Bible. As a Christian, I seek God's direction for my life in the situations I face. As a priest, I am concerned with God's direction for the church. The Bible offers such a broad range of the experience of the people of God seeking the divine will in diverse circumstances that inevitably I can discover therein a situation analogous to my own situation or to the church's. In many spiritual books one encounters the contact of a particular soul with God. In the biblical record one has almost two thousand years of contact with God in very different situations, personal and collective. One of the great thrills of reading the Bible and one of its most attractive features to people who "discover" it is the recognition that the biblical situation is similar to our own. What God demanded by way of response in times past, He is still demanding today.

Q. 19. The description of the Bible as the word of God is not particularly clear. Am I wrong in thinking that "word of God" means different things to different people?

No, I do not think you are wrong. There is ambiguity in the use of the term. All I can tell you is how I understand and use the term with the consciousness that this is what many others involved in biblical studies would say as well.

In analyzing "the word of God" let me begin with the "God" part of the description. What is being said is that this body of work comes from God, or is related to God in a unique way. God supplies guidance in many ways, for example, through the church, through official teaching, through families. And, of course, He supplies guidance, not only in the Christian religion, but in Judaism, and in other religions. God is never silent to those of good faith who seek Him. But in the Judeo-Christian tradition about the Bible God has given this *unique* guidance in preserved written form, which constitutes a record of His dealings with Israel and the Early Church. The Bible is *the library of Israel and the library of the Early Church* that preserves the basic experience that can serve as a guide to the subsequent people of God.

If we turn to the "word" part of the description, we are allowing that there is a human element in the Bible. *People* speak words and make audible sounds, and every word in the Scriptures was written down by a human being. A human being thought of the biblical words, and they reflect meaning and experience in the human author's lifetime. Thus, if I may speak broadly, there is a type of incarnate aspect to the Scriptures: God has conveyed His guidance in and through human words. It is probably the "word" aspect of the description that provokes the diversity of approach as to what "word of God" means. A literalist approach assumes that God dictates almost to the degree that the words themselves come from God and are merely handwritten by the human being. A more subtle form of this has at least a mental dictation by God. The greater degree to which one allows a true human composition and human choice of the words, the more one recognizes the combination of the truly divine and the truly human in the Scriptures. The literalist approach has implications about lack of error and a totality of knowledge in the Bible, including scientific and historical knowledge. Every statement in the Bible must be literally true and complete. The more that one allows a true human element in the Scriptures, the more one can allow for limitations of knowledge and, at times, errors. I am sure that other questions will cause me to expand that observation (see Q. 20–24, 26–27—and 64 on inerrancy).

Q. 20. What do you mean by speaking of the Bible as a library?

Often we speak of "the Bible" in the singular as if it were one book. That pays tribute to the divine origins. Nevertheless, the Bible is a collection of some 70 books. (In the Roman Catholic estimation

73; in the Protestant estimation 66; see Q. 5 above.) But my "library" approach is not concerned only with the number of books; what is important is the recognition that the Bible contains books of different literary genres, written at different times and different places. Perhaps the first Old Testament books took shape 800 or 700 years before Christ, even though some of the traditions that are preserved in them were written hundreds of years earlier; the last New Testament book to be written was probably in the early second century. That is why one tends to estimate a thousand years of written composition. In this period of time, biblical authors would have been facing very different problems and would represent different stages of theological perception that would condition the way in which they reported God's revelation. We are not to assume that the human author saw the whole issue. The part of the issue that was seen by him was shaped by what would be of help to his contemporaries. The idea that God was speaking through the human author. i.e., communicating, does not remove that limitation, because God always deals with people as they are and respects their humanity.

Q. 21. What practical effects result from considering the Bible as a collection of books in a library rather than as one book?

Here terminology has great practical effects. When somebody comes up to me and states, "The Bible says this," my first tendency will be to respond, "Which book of the Bible?" On a given topic, one can have biblical authors responding very differently to the same issue.

Moreover, an approach to the Bible as a library affects the expectation of the readers as they open the pages of a particular author. In a modern library, books are on the shelf according to their subject matter: there is a section for history, for biography, for novels, for drama, for poetry, etc. If one walks into a library and asks for a book, the first question from the librarian will be "What kind of book?" That also is a very important question to ask in reading the Bible. Some of the most serious mistakes of biblical interpretation have flowed from an assumption, quite unwarranted, that all the books of the Bible are history. Today, books have dust jackets that tell the reader the genre of the book, and readers automatically adjust their mindset to an expectation in light of that information. No one picks up a Sherlock Holmes story and expects to read accurate history of a character who lived in London at the end of the last century. The biblical books do not come with dust jackets, and an important task of scholarship is to supply an introduction to each book that helps to identify it. People have wasted time measuring fish gullets in order to prove the historicity of the Book of Jonah. An introduction that tells the reader that this is a parable, not history, saves a good deal of confusion.

Q. 22. Don't we believe any more in the inspiration of the Bible?

Certainly I do. And so far as I know, most centrist biblical scholars would not reject that terminology, provided its implications are understood correctly. The very fact that this question has been asked after I explained that there are books of different kinds or genres in the Bible suggests that the implication of that fact for inspiration is not clear. Often it is thought that inspiration makes everything history. It does not; there can be inspired poetry, drama, legend, fiction, etc. If the Book of Jonah is a parable and not history, then God's inspiration makes it an inspired parable. The truth that it conveys about God's desire to convert all nations to the recognition of His Name and to a moral way of life that will bring them happiness is a truth that we can accept as God's inspired word for us. Inspiration does not mean that we have to believe that a historical figure named Jonah was swallowed by a large fish. We would have to deal with the factuality of that only if the Book of Jonah were inspired history. Similarly, if the first chapters of Genesis are not classified in the branch of the library called science, but in the branch of the library called religious lore and legends, we would still accept the creation of the world by God as the inspired truth conveyed by those chapters. We would not, however, have to accept the Genesis description as a scientific account of the origins of the world. It could be an account that the author learned from the legendary imaginings of his people and of other peoples and that he used to convey the truth he was really interested in, namely, that God is sovereign of all and creator of the universe. Thus there is no contradiction between acceptance of inspiration and acceptance of different literary genres, or forms, or styles in the Bible.

Q. 23. Surely it scandalizes people to hear that not everything told us in the Bible happened literally.

I am not certain how universally true that is, since increasingly we are getting a more sophisticated audience, at least in the First World. I suspect that by osmosis from elementary and high school education, people have already realized that parts of the Bible are not literal accounts of factual history. Whether it scandalizes them when that is said under church auspices probably depends on the way in which it is said.

I have never thought it helpful for someone to get up in a pulpit or classroom and announce that this or that biblical incident never happened. My favorite example of bad taste, bad pedagogy, and perhaps bad theology, is for someone in a church setting to pro-claim, "There were no magi." I know quite well that there are serious reasons for doubting the literal historicity of the incident of the magi in the Matthean infancy narrative (see Q. 54–57 below). Nevertheless, the statement made with absolute surety that there were no magi goes beyond what biblical scholarship can prove. It is very difficult to support with evidence such an absolute negative, and so even on a purely scholarly basis one should not state it. Pedagogically, I do not see how such a negative bit of knowledge can be spiritually helpful to the audience, and making statements in a church setting presumably has the purpose of helping people to grow in knowledge of God. How would they be brought closer to God by knowing that there were no magi? Theologically, such a negative statement distracts from the true import of the story and by implication conveys the idea that this story is primarily con-cerned with communicating facts.

In my judgment, the way to preach or teach the magi story in a religious setting is to present the beautiful Old Testament back-ground of wise men coming from the East bringing God's revelation about Israel. (I'll not go into that background, but it lies in the heart of the Balaam story in the Book of Numbers.) In this way the audience can come to understand Matthew's message that these Gentiles, drawing upon a source of knowledge available to them, namely the reading of the stars, have come to adore God, even if they still require guidance of the Hebrew Scriptures to find out precisely where the King of the Jews has been born. When one shows the audience the extent to which the Matthean infancy story is retelling symbolically stories from the Old Testament, one may be conveying to them by implication that this story of the magi is not literal history. But one has not made a point of the lack of historicity, and one is not distracting from the story's theological value. And so to answer your implied question, I think there is nothing scandalous about preaching or teaching each biblical book in its proper literary genre, history as history, parable as parable, when the preacher or teacher has sensitivity to both the purpose of the book and the purpose of the communication.

Let me point out an implication of this, even if it may not have been an implication of your question. Sometimes, because they fear scandal, some would say that it is better to treat a nonhistorical narrative as history and thus cause no problem. That is a dangerous misconception. God's truth should be served by nothing less than the best of human perception, and we endanger acceptance of divine truth when we teach anybody something that by our best scholarly standards is thought to be false. Sooner or later, those who hear the preacher treating Jonah as if it were history, or the first chapters of Genesis as if they were science, will come to realize the falsity of that presentation and, as a consequence, may reject the inspired divine truth contained in those chapters. In treating any passage of Scripture one need not raise problems that the audience has no way of understanding or of suspecting; but a discreet silence about extremely complicated issues is not the same as teaching or preaching something thought to be false. In preaching the infancy narratives (as distinct from giving a course in a university) I do not go into all the complications of historicity. But neither do I explicitly or implicitly suggest that all the incidents therein are history and must be believed. We probably need to be careful about underestimating the sophistication of the audience. I wonder if one were speaking to a fifth grade grammar school class about the star that rose in the East and came toward Jerusalem and came to settle over Bethlehem, would there not already be on the lips of the children a question as to whether all this happened, or is it "just a story." The challenge to the teacher or preacher may be to walk a middle line between affirming that all this happened literally and suggesting that it is *just* a story. It is a story in which God's inspired truth is communicated to us.

Q. 24. But how far do we go in not taking biblical stories literally? I don't have much problem about the world not being created in six days and life developing by evolution, but what about Adam and Eve? I've heard my pastor state that we have to believe that those are real people.

While sometimes I would like to give pastors equal time by offering them the chance to clarify what they stated, it may well be that your pastor did state exactly that. Certainly when I was in the seminary, I was taught a very literal approach to the existence of Adam and Eve. In part that was because of a response of the Roman Pontifical Biblical Commission at the beginning of the century specifying that certain parts of the Genesis story should be taken literally, including the appearance of the devil in the form of a serpent. We were told that we had to accept as factual that the first woman was formed from the first man and there was a unity to the human race in the sense that all human beings were descended from that first set of parents. If your pastor was trained before 1955, that is probably what he would have been taught. But in 1955 the secretary of the Roman Pontifical Biblical Commission announced that Catholics now had "complete freedom" with regard to those earlier responses of the commission except where they touched faith and morals. Therefore, there was increasing freedom as to the literalness of the Genesis account.

The situation of Adam and Eve, however, was further complicated by the encyclical *Humani Generis* issued by Pope Pius XII in 1950. He mentioned the theory of polygenism, namely that there was more than one set of parents responsible for human beings now existing on the face of the earth; and he said, "it is in no way apparent how such an opinion can be reconciled" with what has been taught on original sin. Some have interpreted that to mean that he condemned polygenism, but that is not what he stated. Many theologians did think that a plural set of parents could be reconciled with original sin and, indeed, even with Paul's description of sin coming into the world through one man in Romans 5. (I'll not try to go into all the exegetical reasoning behind that.) Curiously, though, the scientific situation has shifted. Whereas in the 1950s most scientists would have favored polygenism, genetic discoveries seem now to favor that all human beings are descended from one set of parents.

Perhaps the following could be said. The issue of whether there was one or many sets of parents is partly a scientific issue, and therefore when speaking religiously we should be wary of aligning ourselves too firmly with one or the other scientific position since neither is proved. The genuine religious concern in the Adam and Eve story is that, whether there was one set of parents or more, they were all created by God in the sense that God breathed into them a living soul. Furthermore, they were created good, and not evil, even as we are created good and not evil. Nevertheless, there is in human beings a basic sinful tendency which goes beyond personal sins we may commit; and this basic tendency toward evil is part of the corruption that human beings have introduced into the world, not an endowment by God. Thus we could preserve the core of the concept of "original sin" (even if that terminology is not technically biblical but reflects more the articulation of St. Augustine and other early Church Fathers). We could also recognize how well the ingenious biblical story of Adam and Eve conveyed the idea of sin and its origins and not think that we will find a better modern substitute for telling that story. There is a middle position between what *you heard* your pastor to say by way of insisting on the literal historicity of the Adam and Eve story and a destructive and inaccurate statement, "There were no Adam and Eve."

Q. 25. Whether you take the Adam and Eve story literally or parabolically, does it not do real harm in the sense that it is derogatory to women?

I do not want to be a foolish man rushing in where angels fear to tread; and so while I shall try to respond to the question, I do not wish to open up issues of feminism that go beyond my competence both as a biblical scholar and a man. I think that, when properly understood, the Genesis story is not derogatory to women, even though I do recognize that certain passages in other parts of the Bible may well be derogatory, since they reflect some of the prejudices of the time in which they were written. The creation of the woman from one of the man's ribs described in Gen 2:21 is not designed primarily to show the woman as a secondary figure derivative from the man or lesser than the man. Indeed, Adam's immediate response when he sees the woman in Gen 2:23 is to say that this is "bone of my bone and flesh of my flesh," in other words, someone who is exactly the same as I am—not an animal or an inferior creation. The whole point of the story is an argument against the thesis that woman is merely the chattel of man to be placed on a lower level. The Genesis statement (1:27) that in originating the human race God created male and female in the divine image is an affirmation of the equality of the two sexes before God, mirroring God in a complementary way. One needs to know a bit about the inferior status of women, not only in the surrounding countries but sometimes in the actual practice of Israel, to realize that in a very real way the author of Genesis is correcting inequality and a theology of female inferiority. Thus the Genesis story offers a perceptive preacher or teacher a chance to teach some very basic values about the dignity of both sexes.

Q. 26. Let's not get bogged down in the Adam and Eve story. If one treats that as symbolic or parabolic, where do we stop? Was there an Abraham, or a Moses, or a David, or a Jeremiah? It seems to me that by departing from the literal history of the Bible you have opened a can of worms.

There is no doubt that a totally literal approach is simpler; but in life there are cans of worms and the totally simple answer often doesn't work. Let me remind you of a common experience: after having read home-improvement manuals, those trying to fix the plumbing or the electricity sometimes find themselves utterly frustrated and have to call in the technicians. When they explain to the plumber or the electrician what they did, and complain that it should have worked because this is what they read in the manual, the answer is often: "Ah, but this is a more complicated situation because of these factors which you did not think about." Somehow we can be brought to accept that plumbing, and electricity, and a thousand other aspects of life may be complicated; but we are innately annoyed that the dealings between God and the human race are complicated.

Suppose I were to ask you whether you really think that Washington cut down the cherry tree, or threw a coin across the Potomac, or slept in all the houses in which he is supposed to have bivouacked, you might answer, "Well, I think some of that is legend." How would you then reply if I said to you, "Well, if you begin doubting those things about Washington, how do you know that Lincoln led the Union to victory over the Confederacy, or that Teddy Roosevelt presided over the building of the Panama Canal?" You would soon be forced to recognize that there are different bodies of evidence for different claims and that at times stories about some people are told with a certain legendary atmosphere whereas stories about others are unadornedly factual. The same has to be recognized in the stories associated with the great biblical characters. King Arthur, King William the Conqueror (responsible for the Norman invasion of England), and Queen Elizabeth II are all monarchs associated with British history; but the quality of what we know about each runs the gamut from allegory with some historical details in the case of Arthur, to a general but often not specific history in the case of William the Conqueror, and finally to the ability to construct almost a day-by-day account of the activities of Elizabeth II. So also, the stories pertinent to Abraham have a general historical setting; but he is presented as the father of two peoples, Israel and Ishmael (the Arabs), so there is a somewhat allegorical character to the story. The story of Moses is part of a national epic in which the achievements of the individual and the history of a people are blended. Parts of the story of David probably stem from a court biographer who lived in that period of history and wrote fairly factually. There is history in all three narratives, but varying amounts of history and of detail. That may be a can of worms, but we have a similar can of worms in regard to American history or British history or any other history. We shall have to put up with our annoyance that God has not spared the history of Israel from the same vicissitudes that have afflicted the histories of other nations.

Q. 27. What about archaeological discoveries? Don't they confirm the historicity of large parts of the Bible?

Archaeology gives a mixed picture. Certainly, archaeological discoveries have thrown a great deal of light on biblical customs, social situations, and physical environment. We see the uncovering of cities and houses that the Israelites of the biblical period lived in. Even in the New Testament era, archaeological discoveries have cast light on such practices as crucifixion and burial, as well as on the streets in Jerusalem that Jesus probably walked.

Nevertheless, when it comes to confirming the exact historicity of a biblical event, archaeological finds have not had a uniform thrust. For instance, in the initial excavations of Jericho, the uncovering of walls violently destroyed confirmed for many the biblical account of Joshua's destruction of the walls. More recent techniques, however, have dated the immense destroyed walls to a period much earlier than Joshua and seem to indicate that Jericho was not even occupied at Joshua's time. Some sites mentioned in the biblical account of the invasion of Palestine by the Israelites have, under excavation, shown signs of destruction precisely at the period when most scholars would date the exodus; others have followed the pattern of Jericho in not providing proof of occupation at this time. The notion that archaeology proves the Bible right is inaccurate and misleading. Biblical criticism suggests that some stories that the excavators were hoping to verify were probably not simple history in the first place, and so it is not surprising when what they recount has not been verified by archaeology.

Q. 28. I notice that you and others frequently use the term "biblical criticism." What do you mean by that?

In some ways it is an unfortunate term. In normal English "criticism" involves a negative judgment, and certainly we do not mean a negative attitude toward the Bible. In a less familiar usage, criticism involves a careful reading and analysis of a work. For instance, a newspaper has movie critics and book critics. Very often their judgment on an individual movie or book may be very favorable, but it is an informed judgment that takes into account the various aspects of what is being "criticized" or "critiqued."

In the case of the Bible, there are various forms of biblical criticism. One form evaluates the Bible as literature and takes into account various techniques that the biblical authors use to accomplish their purpose. Are they good writers? If they are telling a story, have they used effective techniques to make that story interesting? If they are giving us a parabolic writing, are the characters in the parable plausible? Another form of biblical criticism is canonical criticism. The individual works in the library of the Bible are part of the canon, that is, the larger collection venerated by the church that involves both the Old Testament and the New. How does what an author wrote in the 6th century B.C. relate to other books written before it and after it? How does it relate to New Testament works that proclaim faith in Jesus Christ? Within the same part of the canon, how are Paul's judgments modified by the fact that they appear alongside the other works that have differing judgments on a particular issue? For instance, Paul is famous for praising the importance of faith over works (that is, the works that accomplish the Jewish Law; Rom 3:28). In remarkably similar terminology, James praises the value of good works and decries a faith that is simply intellectual (Jas 2:24,26). How do these judgments modify each other as a Christian reads the Bible?

Among the many forms of biblical criticism, I have so far named only two. But the criticism most frequently in mind when a scholar speaks of biblical criticism is *historical criticism*. (And, in fact, when you hear me speak simply of criticism, this is usually what I mean.) It involves seeking knowledge about the author

(background, personal situation, goals), about the situation in
which he wrote (what were the problems he was facing?), and about
the readers or hearers to whom he addressed his work (where were
they? what were their problems? what would they have understood?). It also involves a judgment on the nature of the writing—
categorizing a book as belonging to a particular part of the library
that I described in a previous response (Q. 20). In other words,
historical criticism involves asking about a biblical book the same
kind of questions that one would ask about any other book, were
one trying to discover what message was being conveyed in that
book. What did the author really want to say to those to whom he
was writing? Behind all of this, there is the firm conviction that
God's inspiring the Scriptures does not make irrelevant the outlook
and context of the human author. While God knows all things, the
human author does not; and the wording used by a biblical author
does not, therefore, reflect an answer to all questions.

**Q. 29. Even with the use of such "critical" methods by biblical
scholars, it seems to me there are still some very difficult books and
passages in the Bible. What do you consider the most difficult
biblical book?**

You will remember that the New Testament is my primary
field of study, and so I will respond to that question by modifying it
and asking: What is the most difficult New Testament book? Even
there, I would be inclined to distinguish further as to whether you
mean from the scholar's viewpoint or the reader's viewpoint. But let
me take the reader's viewpoint, since you ask the question. I suppose the most difficult book in the New Testament for the reader is
the Book of Revelation or the Apocalypse. I do not find it terribly
difficult from a scholar's viewpoint because the scholar tends to
have read other books of this same type—Jewish apocalypses filled
with vivid imagery symbolic of good and evil. Therefore, the
scholar is alerted not to take the imagery of the Apocalypse literally,
but to read it as Jews familiar with this type of literature would have
read it when it was written.

Even though we use the term "apocalyptic" today for ominous

and extravagant events, the literary genre of apocalypse in the biblical style is not a familiar form of contemporary writing. Therefore the current reader tends to pick up a book like the Apocalypse or Revelation of John and to take literally various numerical schemata and predictions of an end at hand. This produces enormous confusion. So from that point of view, I would say the Book of Revelation is perhaps the most difficult. I have over the years recommended very strongly a pamphlet published by the Knights of Columbus entitled *Revelation*. Although it does not bear the author's name, it was written by an excellent biblical scholar, Father Bruce Vawter, and in a short span is very helpful for understanding the message of the Apocalypse.

Q. 30. In light of that answer about difficulty, what is the message of the Apocalypse or the Book of Revelation?

I am delighted that your question caught my use of two names under which the book is known. Perhaps I should say three names because many people ask me about the Book of Revelations—a plural that is incorrect and, indeed, can give a wrong direction, for it supposes a group of revelations to the author. The name "Apocalypse" is almost a transliteration of the Greek *Apokalypsis,* and means unveiling. "Revelation" is almost a transliteration of the Latin equivalent *Revelatio* which also means an unveiling. Thus there is implied a knowledge of what hitherto was covered over or hidden.

You asked me about the message. Let me first state very precisely what it is not. We need not suppose the author had or was given by God knowledge of the distant future. Therefore, useless are all speculations about how long the earth is to last, or how long it will be before Christ comes back, or when the end of the world will come—speculations based on the Book of Revelation, or on the Book of Daniel which has another set of apocalyptic visions. Nevertheless, these speculations have haunted people for 2,000 years, as in the course of time various individuals have jumped up with the Book of Revelation in their hand and announced that they now understand the numerical message and the end time is at hand.

Thus far all such interpretations have been wrong: the world is still here.

The basic message of the Apocalypse is one of hope in a time of persecution. Using symbolic language, such as that of great beasts, dragons, floods, fire, etc., the author describes his time as one of severe affliction and suffering produced by evil. Amidst this, he wishes to reassure the readers that God has control of all things, whence his imagery of a heavenly book in which all things are written down, or of a period of time in which the various activities that happen have a set limit, or of angels that can overcome the forces of evil, or even of good beasts that can overcome the bad beasts. He is saying to the persecuted and suffering group that they are not to despair, for God will bring all this to an end and be victorious. He will save those who have remained faithful and destroy the forces of evil. When will all of this happen? Soon. And one can say "soon" whether writing 500 years before Christ (Ezekiel), or 250 years before Christ (Daniel), or at the end of the first Christian century (Apocalypse and Jewish writings like *IV Ezra*). The "soon" is from God's standpoint and is to be met by our firm conviction that God does not allow His people to be trampled on and destroyed indefinitely.

There is also a more profound message that I will mention only briefly. There is a conviction that what happens on earth so visibly by way of wars, persecutions, and catastrophes is but a pale and insignificant part of total reality. Far more important is what goes on in heaven, in terms both of the praise of God by myriads of angels and saints, and of God's victory over supernatural forces of evil (for instance, Michael over Satan). An apocalyptic writer often sees the heavenly at the same time as the earthly, and brings to the readers a sense of a wider reality beyond that of the cosmic. The magnificent liturgies in heaven are part of reality if we have the eyes of faith to perceive them. And so there is an obligation on earth to participate in the heavenly and not to set our total concern on what we can see and touch with our senses. The mystical, the otherworldly, the celestial are all part of the gift of apocalyptic to the broader picture of Christian faith and understanding. That is why I feel it is such a travesty when in a work like Revelation fundamentalists search primarily for keys to present local history. Often they are missing the whole point of the mystical dimension.

Q. 31. In responding to the question on the Book of Revelation you used the term fundamentalists. That interests me because I find this is an increasing problem as I associate with others interested in the Bible. Even if I encounter people who are said to be fundamentalists, I am not totally clear what the term means.

You are perfectly correct in recognizing that contact with fundamentalism is an increasing problem, and I would say a *new* problem especially for Roman Catholics. If I may indulge in a moment of history, so far as I know, the origin of the term "fundamentalism" came at the beginning of this century, just after 1910. At that time, under the impact of biblical criticism—and I told you that that most often means historical criticism—there had been a considerable loss of faith in the supernatural in the Scriptures. After all, when one begins asking of the biblical books the same questions one asks of other books, the element of God's word may be obscured, especially if one does not have a firm faith in their divine origin. In this situation two wealthy Southern Californians sponsored a series of pamphlets designed to defend the *fundamentals* of the Christian religion, namely such doctrines as the virginal conception, the miracles of Jesus, the resurrection, the divinity of Christ, hell, and an anti-Darwinian view of creation.

I mention the last as a caution. While Catholics would share the concern of the original fundamentalists about the essentials of the Christian faith, we would be able to distinguish between holding on to the doctrine of creation and a view of creation that rejected evolution. The last would not be seen to us as a fundamental of the Christian faith. Moreover, since this reaction came within the confines of Protestantism, some of what Roman Catholics would have called upon as support for these doctrines, for instance, creeds and the traditions of the church, could not be invoked. The whole effort was to prove the doctrines from the Bible, with the understanding that the only way this could be done was to maintain the literal meaning of the Bible. The contention was that any departure from the literal historicity of all parts of the Bible opened the way to a loss of faith in the fundamentals.

I have intended to be brief in my response to this question, so I do not wish to go into the differences between fundamentalists and evangelicals. For all practical purposes, what your question presupposes and what my answer presupposes is *a literalist reading of the Bible to support Christian doctrine.* I applaud some of the doctrinal stress of fundamentalists but I disagree thoroughly with the method they employ. In my judgment, a literalist reading of the Bible is intellectually indefensible and is quite unnecessary for the defense of the basic Christian doctrines.

A helpful, very short pamphlet to give someone who is first encountering fundamentalist Bible reading is *Understanding the Bible* (Christopher News Notes 313; March 1989).

Q. 32. But why are fundamentalists now becoming a more notice-able problem? It seems to me that we never had to deal with these people before.

I think that, for the most part, modern fundamentalism understood as defensive literalist interpretation of the Bible is an American phenomenon. I know that it has spread to other countries; but the main area from which it draws its nourishment is the United States—indeed more specifically the southern half of the United States. In this country, before the 1960s, Roman Catholics lived in the large cities of the North where often they were a majority. They did not enter into Protestant churches or hear Protestant sermons. Therefore, they were unaffected either geographically or existentially by Protestant fundamentalism. After the 1960s, with the large migrations to the "Sun Belt," Catholics moved en masse into the South, the Southwest, and the West Coast; and there they did encounter fundamentalists.

Moreover, this was the great moment of media development; and so even without entering Protestant churches, they could turn on their radios or their televisions in the Sun Belt area and hear the Bible being explained by fundamentalists. I saw figures some years ago that over a thousand radio stations and some 65–70 television stations in the South were in the hands of biblical fundamentalists. It was also the moment of the entrance of Catholics into the American mainstream. Before 1960 in an isolated situation that was almost a religious ghetto, Catholics could develop a spirituality based on lives of the saints, *The Imitation of Christ,* and the devotional writings of Francis de Sales and Thérèse of Lisieux (for which I have the highest respect). But in mainstream America the Bible is the sole *lingua franca* of religion—the only way in which faith, doctrine, and spirituality is traditionally phrased. As our heritage from Elizabethan and Puritan England we were, after all, a Protestant republic in which Catholics were immigrants or resident aliens.

Now it should be remembered that careful exposition of the Bible really has not been a major formative element in Catholic religious life. I know there has been a greater emphasis on preaching the Scriptures since the renewal of the liturgy and the revision of the lectionary we use on Sundays, but still I would judge that most preaching and catechetical teaching is not intensively biblical. Yet the Bible is interesting, fascinating, and captivating when people hear it. So when, beginning in the 60s on the fundamentalist media, Catholics were hearing the Bible explained, even if it was explained in a literalist way, their attention was caught. They found themselves saying, Why did I never hear this before? *And that is an honest question we should wrestle with.* The fact that in the South their neighbors sometimes went to Bible classes or had Bible readings in their homes often attracted them as well, if they wanted to become part of the neighborhood. And, of course, where the majority of the population consists of biblical literalists, these Bible readings would be fundamentalist.

To counteract this massive exposure, we have had very little means—and, indeed, neither have the mainline Protestant churches, which have lost tremendous numbers of people to fundamentalist groups. Very often the Catholic Church is a minority presence in the Sun Belt area; the clergy and the teachers are not well trained biblically; there has been no massive Catholic emphasis on presenting the Bible on the media. (We may have masses said and televised; but an intelligent, modern biblical presentation with a pastoral goal is a real lack. Pious comments on biblical passages are not what I am talking about.) There are probably many other factors of a social and even political nature that could be added, but at least I have tried to explain to you why the attraction of biblical literalists has suddenly become a major factor in Catholic life.

Q. 33. How would you counteract this biblical fundamentalism?

That is an immense subject; I can only outline some suggestions.

1. Do not waste time arguing over individual biblical texts with fundamentalists. The question is a much larger one of overall views of religion, of Christianity, and of the nature of the Bible.

2. Do not attack fundamentalists as if they were fools or ignorant. Often, biblical literalism is an attitude of self-defensiveness for even extremely intelligent people who have been trapped. They want to preserve their faith in God, and this seems to them the only way. They will understand your attacks on them as an attack on their faith. There can be fundamentalists very well-informed in biblical archaeology and languages. They will have developed apologetic arguments against any nonliteral positions. For example, if one is against evolution, one can argue that God created the world with fossils already in it and, therefore, that the fossil proof for evolution can be dismissed!

3. If you encounter a convinced fundamentalist, beware of trying to convert that person too suddenly away from fundamentalism. The result may not be the fundamentalist's adherence to a more centrist Christian view, but a complete loss of faith. The more important goal is not to devastate fundamentalists, but to offer those who have not already been swallowed up by fundamentalism a richer faith and a more intelligent presentation of the Bible.

4. That last remark leads me into the key step we must take. The Bible must be presented intelligently and in a nonliteralist fashion on the media, in the churches, in Bible classes, etc. If people want to know about the Bible, and the only ones who offer them a chance to know about it are the fundamentalists, they will go to the fundamentalists. I do not care how rich the liturgy is, how firm the catechism is, how marvelous the personal devotions are—if the

Bible is left out, the situation is dangerous. It is dangerous on the American scene in particular, where, as I explained, the Bible is the *lingua franca* of religion. Here, unless one can talk biblically, one cannot talk religiously. This is dangerous on a personal level because the Bible has such tremendous attractiveness that it cannot simply be counteracted, nor should it be, by substitution.

5. There is a shortage of Catholic priests and many Catholic priests are not good expositors of the Bible. At the same time there is a real interest among the laity, and they should be tapped for this service. But they have to be informed, and that task requires people with education to supply some of the basic starting insights. If as a church we recognize this as a major problem, then we should mobilize our forces in order to supply intelligent biblical leadership among Catholics. That will prevent them from becoming fundamentalists. I do not think we have done this as a church. We are very aware of trying to meet the challenge of overliberalism or of secularism. We do not sufficiently see the danger to the right.

6. This is not a danger that affects Roman Catholics alone. There is no reason why the mainline Protestant churches and Roman Catholics cannot join in a common effort to present the Bible intelligently. Some of the Protestant churches have already developed excellent aids for reading the Bible. The fear of loss of Roman Catholic doctrine if we cooperate with Protestants is largely exaggerated. Indeed, were the media cooperation sponsored by various church leaders, I think they would recognize that the essential issue is to communicate a basic intelligent approach to the Bible that respects Christian doctrines on which we all agree.

7. There are accompanying elements in fundamentalism that make it attractive. Fundamentalists often have a strong sense of community, and they lovingly care for those who participate in the fundamentalist church or group. We should be aware that with our large Roman Catholic parishes, often handling several thousand people on a Sunday, we do not have that same sense of community. We may have to break those parishes down, at least functionally, into smaller groups. This was not so necessary in the cities of the North where there was a lot of impersonality in the lifestyle on all levels. But in the more folksy and overtly friendly atmosphere of the Sun Belt, we are not going to be convincing if the fundamentalists

out-brother and out-sister us. Community is a value, and perhaps we can learn it from them.

8. The fundamentalists often proclaim a vivid love of Jesus. Roman Catholics once did quite well on that, in our popular devotions. We may have lost some of that ethos in the laudable development of liturgical language that is less emotional. Nevertheless, the love of Jesus is an enormous attraction within Christianity. When people encounter it, and it seizes them emotionally, it sweeps them off their feet. There is no reason on earth why the love of Jesus cannot be proclaimed by the mainline churches with an equal sense of appropriateness. It was not to a fundamentalist, but to Peter, that in John 21 Jesus three times placed the demand, "Do you love me?" For ordination or for preaching, if we made that a requirement, as Jesus did before he entrusted any of his sheep to Peter's care, perhaps we could also match the fundamentalists in getting people to realize that neither works nor faith without the love of Jesus constitutes the whole Christian picture.

(See also the Appendix below on expressing Catholic faith and fundamentalism.)

Q. 34. So far you have been responding to questions on the Bible in general with many references to the Old Testament. Isn't the New Testament different? It was not written hundreds of years after the events it describes, but almost contemporaneously. Surely we can trust its historicity.

Your question reminds me of a professor who once taught in a seminary where I was. He always insisted that you could apply form criticism to the Old Testament but not to the New. I think he understood form criticism to mean a diminution of historicity, whereas of course it means diagnosing the literary character or genre of a particular book—the "library" approach that I spoke of previously (see Q. 20). Like the Old Testament, the New Testament is also a library, namely, the library of the Early Church. When you say that surely we can trust its historicity, that might imply that all twenty-seven books are histories and, of course, they are not. One can scarcely speak of history in regard to the symbolic visions of the Book of Revelation that I pointed out (see Q. 29–30).

Many of the New Testament works are epistles or letters. Again, applying a measure of historicity to them has its difficulties. Presumably, of course, the letter writer is not inventing the situation to which he is addressing himself; but the evaluation of the letter would far more appropriately concern the quality of the message rather than its historicity. As for these letters being contemporaneous with the events they describe, one must face the issue that while some of the letters attributed to Paul were undoubtedly written by him, others were probably written by his disciples, in his name, even after his death. In relation to other New Testament letters attributed to Peter, and to James, and to Jude, a similar problem exists. Perhaps with the New Testament one does not have all the acute problems of historicity that one has in dealing with the Old Testament narratives, but there are problems in the New Testament as well.

Q. 35. How can anyone who believes in inspiration raise the issue of the genuine character of Paul's letters? The New Testament says that Paul wrote them.

Perhaps I could begin by distinguishing between what the New Testament says and what it does not say. I have heard lectionary readers in church begin a passage by identifying it as coming from "St. Paul's Letter to the Hebrews." If one looks at the New Testament, there is no clear indication that the Epistle to the Hebrews was written by St. Paul; and indeed in the text there is no reference "to the Hebrews." The identification of this letter as one written "to the Hebrews" comes in the second century (not in the biblical text itself), and the identification of the author as Paul comes even later and for a while only in part of the church. The Roman church was most reluctant to accept this as a letter of Paul. Similarly, one speaks of three letters of John. But there is no reference whatsoever to John in the text of those letters; once more that is a guess stemming from the second century rather than from the New Testament.

Yet you do have a point about other letters that specifically identify their author. Thirteen of the New Testament works are letters that bear the name of Paul in the text. Of those thirteen, scholars overwhelmingly attribute seven to Paul's own composition: I Thessalonians, Galatians, I–II Corinthians, Philippians, Philemon, and Romans. Perhaps 90% of critical scholarship thinks that Paul did not himself compose the Pastoral Epistles (I–II Timothy, Titus); perhaps 80% would agree that he did not write Ephesians; perhaps 60% that he did not write Colossians; and slightly over half that he did not write II Thessalonians. I give you my guesses about the percentage of scholarship to stress that this is not an absolute science; nevertheless, we are dealing with the opinions of more than a few. Similarly, in relation to the Catholic Epistles, perhaps 95% would agree that Peter did not compose II Peter; perhaps 75% that Jude did not compose Jude, or that James did not compose James; and it would be a toss-up among scholars whether Peter had a hand in I Peter.

Does not inspiration guarantee that when an epistle has the name of Paul or Peter, that figure wrote it? Absolutely not, any more than the fact that Moses is said to have written the Pentateuch guarantees that Moses wrote it. There is a convention of attributing works appropriately to a great authority. Moses was remembered as one who received the Law, and therefore legal material was attributed to Moses as its author. Solomon was remembered as a wise man, and therefore wisdom material was attributed to Solomon. David was remembered as a singer of psalms; and therefore one can speak of the psalter of David, even though some of the psalms are specifically not attributed to David in that psalter. Similarly, after Paul had died and disciples in his tradition wished to instruct people about what Paul's mind would have been in facing new situations, they felt free to write under the mantle of Paul. As I have insisted previously, writing is a human activity; and divine inspiration respects the conventions of that activity.

To give you an example of how Catholic scholarship has developed on this subject, let me turn to *The Jerusalem Bible* that I mentioned in response to a previous question (Q. 2). In the original English form of *The Jerusalem Bible* one found this: "Some critics have concluded that the [Pastoral] Letters were written not by Paul, but by a forger who put in these details to make the letter seem more authentic and as Pauline as possible." In commenting on that Bible I strongly protested the prejudicial character of such a remark which ignored the convention of writing in someone else's name (i.e., pseudonymity). In *The New Jerusalem Bible* I was delighted to find: "The best explanation may be that the Pastoral Epistles are letters written by a follower of Paul, conscious of inheriting his mantle and seeking to give advice and instruction for the administration of local churches. This adoption of a revered name in such circumstances was a literary convention of the times." To my mind that represents the development of Catholic critical scholarship from the 1950s to the 1980s.

Q. 36. Your answer implies that it does not make too much difference whether Paul himself or a disciple wrote a particular letter. Then let me turn the question around: Why do scholars waste time determining whether or not Paul wrote a letter?

My answer was not intended to give the implication that it made no difference as to meaning whether or not Paul wrote a letter. I was answering only the question of whether a proper theory of inspiration would allow us to say that Paul did not write a letter that opened with the words, "From Paul, by the will of God an apostle of Christ Jesus . . . ," and my answer was yes.

Contrary to the implication you found, I think it makes an enormous difference whether or not Paul wrote a letter. Our picture of how the Early Church developed can be greatly influenced by the decision about authorship. If the Pastoral Epistles were written by Paul during his lifetime, that means that a massive concentration on church structure and who should be presbyter-bishops, and how teaching should be controlled was already a factor in the early 60s. If the vast majority of scholars are correct and Paul did not write this letter, this issue arose precisely because the apostolic generation of which Paul was a representative had now died out and therefore there was a problem of who should have the responsibility for pastoring and teaching Christian churches.

If Colossians and Ephesians were written by Paul during his

lifetime, his theology had shifted remarkably in the sense that ecclesiology had now come to the fore, almost replacing christology as
the main emphasis. These two letters are concerned with *the* church
as the body of Christ for which he gave himself. While in his genuine letters Paul stresses to Christians that they are all members of
the body of Christ, the collective view of the church, almost as the
end and goal of Christ's work, is not emphasized as it is in Colossians and Ephesians. We are asking then just where in the trajectory
of early Christian development ecclesiology began to come to the
fore. I can give many other examples of the importance of authorship issues.

Q. 37. If Paul did not write these letters, even if they are inspired, do they have less authority?

I would give a firm no to that question, even though I know
that implicitly many scholars, including Catholic scholars, write in
that vein. I mentioned that issues of church structure, especially the
necessity for presbyter-bishops, are the subject of the Pastoral Epistles. Some who would reconstruct today a church without eccle-
siastical authority, or with less authority, or with a desire to introduce sweeping changes about the nature of authority, would argue
that these letters were not written by Paul and therefore are not so
important.

You posed your question by asking, even if the letters not
written by Paul were *inspired,* did that mean that they had the same
authority as genuine letters. I would trace my positive answer not
simply to inspiration but to the nature of the canon. In accepting
these letters into the canon, the Christian community has bound
itself to live by them and their authority. I hope I have made clear
that I have no fundamentalist understanding of revelation or of
scriptural authority, but I see another type of fundamentalism on
the part of those who can simply dismiss canonical works or their
importance on the dubious grounds of authorship. The church's
commitment to the Scriptures as a foundational norm of its life is a
more important issue than that of which author in the Early Church
wrote a particular work. If one insists on apostolic authorship

(which for all practical purposes would mean authorship before the mid 60s), most of the New Testament would lose its authority. The author of the Pastorals was dealing with a situation that Paul did not face head-on in his lifetime. The answer that he gives to that situation in Paul's name deserves far more respect than imaginative modern reconstructions of what Paul thought in his lifetime—reconstructions that are not based on hard data and are usually the reflection of what a scholar would like Paul to have thought.

Q. 38. When you were asked about the historicity of the New Testament, you responded largely in terms of Paul's letters and their authorship. What about the Gospels? How reliable are their portraits of Jesus?

Very often an overall response is that the Gospels are not biographies, and in general that is true. Normally a biographer has the primary intention of writing a full life of an individual, recording all that we can know about him or her. Two of the Gospels (Mark and John) tell us nothing about Jesus' origins, birth, or early life before his encounter with John the Baptist. Mark never mentions the name of Jesus' legal father (Joseph) and John never mentions the name of his mother (Mary—yes, he speaks of "the mother of Jesus" but he never gives us her name; if we had only John, we would not know Mary's name). Those lacunae exemplify the absence from the Gospels of a considerable amount of biographical material that should have been included were the evangelists writing biographies of Jesus.

Yet I would point out that, while in general the Gospels are not biographies, the Gospel According to Luke, since it is joined to the Book of Acts, which narrates a loose type of history of the early Christians, and since it does have a story of Jesus' conception, birth, and youth, would come closer to the appearance of a biography than any of the other Gospels. Also, while no Gospel gives us a complete or dispassionate account of Jesus' life, all the Gospels give us some historical data about the circumstances of his life, his words, and his deeds. Therefore the statement that the Gospels are not biographies does not in any way rule out that their portraits are more than simply theological evaluations—they are interpretations of a real life, real words, and real deeds.

Q. 39. I was brought up reading lives of Christ in school and on retreats. You just mentioned that it was a real life that he lived. Nevertheless, it seems to me that we see very few lives of Christ today. When did this approach change?

Your question correctly assumes a connection between treating the Gospels as biographies and writing lives of Christ. If the Gospels are not considered biographical or simply historical, there will be much less tendency to gather what we know of Jesus into a "life," for scholars will acknowledge that gaps in the evidence frustrate that goal. As for when we started taking a less biographical approach and thus thinking less immediately of lives of Christ, the answer depends to a certain extent on who the "we" are. The change of approach to the Gospels is a result of modern biblical criticism, and distinguished Protestants scholars were already employing criticism in relation to the Gospels in the last century. (For what I mean by criticism, I remind you of a previous answer: Q. 28 above.) Roman Catholics came latterly into the acceptance of a modern critical approach to the New Testament and to the Gospels. Yet, as often happens, when after prolonged hesitation we Catholics accept new approaches, we proceed with an official church statement of our position. Protestants were using these methods long before they were accepted by Catholics, but Protestant churches have not made the same kind of official commitment to them that the Roman Catholic Church has.

In particular, in the period just before Vatican II and during the Council, there was an active and even acrimonious debate in official Catholic circles about the Gospels and their historicity. This culminated in 1964 when the Pontifical Biblical Commission (at that time an official organ of Church teaching with binding authority when approved by the Pope) issued a document on "The Historical Truth of the Gospels." (An essential part of this is reprinted in my *Biblical Reflections on Crises Facing the Church* [New York: Paulist, 1975, pp. 111–115].) The scholars who contributed to the document were attempting to put together a centrist approach, drawing on their Protestant and Catholic confreres. They gave a picture of Gospel development that led to the conclusion that the Gospels are not literal accounts of the ministry of Jesus nor do they report material simply that it might be remembered. I am very sympathetic with that phrasing, and I think many other New Testament scholars would be also.

Q. 40. Could you be more specific? If you say the Gospels are not literal accounts of the ministry of Jesus and they are not biographies, what are they? How should we understand them?

I shall not hide from you that scholars might answer that in different ways. But the response that I will give will be phrased in terms of the outline supplied by the document of the Roman Pontifical Biblical Commission mentioned in the last response. Then at least you can see how a whole committee of scholars approached the question, and that my response is in harmony with an official stance accepted by the Roman Catholic Church. This response may be a bit long, but I think you can follow it if I spell out from the beginning that there are three stages in a development of tradition about Jesus that led to the production of Gospels.

In STAGE ONE the process began with Jesus' public life: the period of activity in Galilee and environs where he preached and healed. This approach insists that Jesus did things of note and that he orally proclaimed his message, so that followers (especially those who traveled with him, some of whom would later be known as apostles) heard and saw what he said and did. It is very important to emphasize that his were the words and deeds of one who lived as a Galilean Jew in the first third of the first century; his manner of speaking, the problems he faced, his vocabulary and outlook were those of a Galilean Jew of that specific time. Many of the failures to understand Jesus and the misapplications of his thoughts stem from the fact that people remove him from space and time and imagine that he was dealing with issues that he never encountered.

STAGE TWO in the development of the Jesus tradition that eventually produced the Gospels consisted of a preaching phase that occurred after the death and resurrection of Jesus. If one wants to assign chronological perimeters to these stages, I have already assigned the first third of the century to Stage One, and I would assign the second third of the first century (roughly to 65) to this preaching in Stage Two. Those who had heard and seen Jesus had their general acceptance of him confirmed through the resurrection and came to believe in him under various titles (Messiah/Christ, Lord, Savior, Son of God, etc.). In proclaiming him, they developed further the story of what they had heard and seen under the influence of the faith they now possessed, which illumined for them the significance of those past events. Thus there was no attempt to report with simple, uncolored factuality what Jesus had said and done. Rather the report was enlightened by a faith that the preachers wanted to share.

Inevitably others who had not heard and seen Jesus joined in this proclamation in dependence on what they received from the original witnesses, so that the preaching was a combination of eye-witness and non-eyewitness narration. We are not guessing at that: in I Cor 15, Paul after referring to a set formula of the Jesus tradition concerning death, burial, resurrection, and appearance (15:3–5), mentions Cephas (Peter) and the Twelve (who would have been eyewitnesses) and also mentions himself (and he had not been an eyewitness of the ministry of Jesus). Then he says to the audience of his letter: "Whether then it was I or they, so we preach and so you believed."

Another factor, besides the enrichment supplied by faith and the entrance of non-eyewitnesses into the preaching, was the necessary adaptation of the preaching to a new audience. If Jesus was a Galilean Jew of the first third of the first century, the Gospel was preached in cities to urban Jews and Gentiles; it was preached eventually in Greek, a language that Jesus did not normally speak in Galilee (if he spoke it at all). All of this meant a good deal of translation in the broader sense of the term, and this translation designed to make the message both intelligible and alive for new audiences was part of the development of the Gospel tradition.

STAGE THREE involved the actual writing of the Gospels as we now know them. This stage I will date to the last third of the first century, fixing Mark about 70, Matthew and Luke in the period

80–90, and John in the 90s—all of this an approximation, give or take ten years. Sections of the Jesus tradition were probably already in writing before the evangelists composed their respective Gospels, but none of that pre-Gospel writing has been preserved for us. A key to understanding Stage Three is that most likely none of the evangelists was himself an eyewitness of the ministry of Jesus. All were what we may call second-generation Christians: They had heard about Jesus from others and were organizing the tradition they had received into a written Gospel. That insight saves us from an enormous number of problems that bedeviled an earlier generation of commentators who thought that some of the evangelists had themselves seen what they reported. In that previous approach a John who reports the cleansing of the Temple at the beginning of the ministry in chapter 2 and a Matthew who reports the cleansing of the Temple at the end of the ministry in chapter 21 had to be reconciled by maintaining that the cleansing happened twice, and that each evangelist chose to report only one of the two instances. In the approach I am proposing, where neither writer was an eyewitness, each received a form of the story of the cleansing of the Temple from the Jesus tradition; neither one may have known when it actually occurred during the ministry, since he was not there; but each included it in the written Gospel in the position where it best served the plan of the Gospel. I could give ten other instances of where the eyewitness approach to the evangelists causes theories of doubling or other implausible explanations, and where the non-eyewitness approach offers a very simple solution; for it explains well Gospels that frequently contain the same material but just as frequently have that material arranged in entirely different ways. The end product of this is the judgment that the Gospels are in logical order, not necessarily in chronological order. Each evangelist has ordered the material according to his understanding of Jesus and his desire to portray Jesus in a way that would meet the spiritual needs of the community to which he was addressing the Gospel. Thus the individual evangelists emerge as full authors of the Gospels, shaping, developing, pruning the tradition, and as full theologians, orienting that tradition to a particular goal.

Thus in overall response to the question about what the Gospels are, I would describe a Gospel as containing a distillation from the tradition about Jesus, involving his words, deeds, passion, death, and resurrection. This distillation was organized, edited, and reshaped by an evangelist in the last third of the first century in order to address the spiritual needs of Christian readers he envisaged. That is why the document of the Roman Pontifical Biblical Commission from which I have drawn this outline of three stages can evaluate the Gospels as historical but not as an exact memory or a literal account.

Q. 41. What practical effect has the modern approach to the Gospels as the product of developing tradition had for our spiritual use of the Gospels?

Let me answer by a practical example. One needs simply to turn to the Sunday Lectionary (that collection of Old Testament and New Testament readings that we use in church for liturgies), a lectionary that in its broad lines is now accepted by many different Christian churches. In the Roman Catholic Church, before the current lectionary was introduced, one heard the same 52 passages on the Sundays of every year. Those passages were intermingled without distinction from the Gospels, so that one Sunday the parishioners might have heard a passage from Matthew, and another Sunday from Luke, but rarely from Mark. Very often in my experience as a priest, one might have preached on a passage such as the parable of the sower without ever emphasizing which Gospel it came from. That was because both preacher and audience had the impression that the individual Gospel background made no difference in the meaning of the passage—Jesus had spoken the parable, and the evangelists were only reporters.

In the new three-year lectionary, however, the Gospel readings are from Matthew in the first year, from Mark in the second year, and Luke in the third year. The Gospel readings from John are at specified times, like Lent and Easter. That organization recognizes the great importance of localizing a particular pericope (i.e., the Gospel passage of the day) in the Gospel from which it was taken, because the context of the whole Gospel lends meaning to the pericope. For example, the story of the multiplication of the loaves occurs in all four Gospels; but it can have a different meaning in each according to the logic of the evangelist. Perhaps not all preachers are aware of this; yet the organization of the lectionary urges them to be aware of it.

Q. 42. You have said that the evangelists were not eyewitnesses. We were taught that Matthew and John wrote Gospels, and these were certainly eyewitnesses of the ministry of Jesus.

That is a reaction that I often get from Catholics and a very understandable reaction because we were taught exactly those identifications, at least up until about 1960. In the early 1900s the Roman Pontifical Biblical Commission issued official answers to a number of questions that had been provoked by the development of critical biblical scholarship, particularly among Protestants. It insisted that substantially the Gospel that appears first in the New Testament represented the work (perhaps in translation) of Matthew, one of the Twelve, and that the Fourth Gospel was the work of John, one of the Twelve. (There were also solutions commanded for Old Testament questions: Moses wrote the Pentateuch; Isaiah was one book; Daniel was written in the sixth century B.C.)

In the mid-1950s, however, as I mentioned before (Q. 24), the secretary of the same Roman Pontifical Biblical Commission explained that now Catholics had full freedom with regard to such decrees except when they touched on faith and morals (and really none of them did that in any substantial way). That means that while earlier Catholic teaching about the identity of the evangelists was bound by an official church response, that is no longer the case. Catholics are now as free as anyone else to express their views about the identity of the evangelists. By the way, the somewhat embarrassing public change of mind about a strongly enforced position underlines the danger of invoking church authority to settle what are basically scientific questions—questions not about doctrine but about authorship, date, and composition. Faith and morals are the restricted area in which the Spirit guides the church.

The view that the evangelists were not themselves eyewitnesses of the public ministry of Jesus would be held in about 95% of contemporary critical scholarship. The 1964 decree of the Roman Biblical Commission (Q. 40 above) did not enter into the identity of the evangelists, although it described them very clearly as different from those who preached in Stage Two and thus implicitly created a distinction between the evangelists and the preachers, some of whom had been companions of Jesus. Yet I should alert you that the church has continued and most likely will continue to use the ancient designation "apostles and apostolic men" for describing the authors of the Gospels, not by way of teaching that they were eye-witnesses, but by way of emphasizing the connection between their works and the apostolic eyewitness.

Let me add that the designations that you find in your New Testament, such as "The Gospel According to Matthew" (note that the oldest designation is "According to" and not "of"), are the results of late-second-century scholarship attempting to identify the authors of works that had no identification. No evangelist indicated who he was. The closest one comes to that in the Gospels is the indication in the Fourth Gospel that an eyewitness, "the disciple whom Jesus loved," was the source of what is written in the Gospel (John 21:24), but then that Gospel never identifies the disciple whom Jesus loved. In the first century, if the question "Whose Gospel is this?" were proposed, what is written at the beginning of the Gospel that we now know as the Gospel According to Mark might be the key. That evangelist wrote "The beginning of the Gospel of Jesus Christ."

Q. 43. You described an approach where the tradition that came from Jesus was modified and developed in stages before the Gospels. Are we not involved in the same type of development ever since when we apply the Gospels to our own time?

I would answer that cautiously. The three stages of development culminating in the written Gospels that I have described (Q. 40) produced books that God in His providence supplied for the guidance of Christians for all ages—in shorthand, inspired books. Once those books of Scripture were produced, they represented a definitive stage of the Jesus tradition, i.e., definitive in the sense that all subsequent generations would use them as its key to what Jesus said and did, and therefore in the sense that these books constitute the norm for Christian belief. There is no doubt that each generation of Christians must continue the process of translating, adapting, and keeping alive Jesus' message for new times. But we do that by reflecting on the written Gospels or on the New Testament (or on the Bible); we do not produce new Scriptures. Of course, we produce new books (even as the church produces new statements) embodying current interpretations of Jesus in the light of new questions; but none of those will acquire the same status as the Gospels of the first century. They will not be regarded as inspired by God in the way in which the Scriptures are. Thus I see at work today a similar process of thought, reflection, and development, but the post-Gospel process is determined by the written Gospels as a norm and guide in a unique way.

Nevertheless, your question does catch some of the implications of our current approach to the Gospels. It is interesting to reflect on the two approaches to the Gospels that I have contrasted, and what type of Christians they might produce. In a biographical approach where the Gospels are in verbatim correspondence with what Jesus did and said, so that there has been no development from his time to that of the evangelists, the clear (and really the only) function of preaching and proclamation is preservation: to take what Jesus said and did and repeat it, without addition, without subtraction, and without modification in each decade. In the approach I have outlined, where there is development, modification, selection, etc., then in each stage there was a contribution. Christians who understand this will see that they must make a contribution in their time to the proclamation and understanding and development of the message about Jesus (but now in dependence on the written Gospels, as I have said). These two approaches, then, produce different Christian models: one is of simple, unchanging preservation; the other is of constant growth and adaptation *while preserving*. Those who are dominated by the first model will be enormously threatened by change, since that could interfere disastrously with preservation and modify the under-

standing of the tradition. Those dominated by the second model are
more likely to see in change new opportunities of interpreting and
comprehending the whole of Jesus' message and its implications.

Obviously, I think of the latter approach as more faithful to
tremendous innovations that Jesus himself made. I like to tell the
story that once I visited a diocese that for a special year was celebrat-
ing Christian teaching and evangelization and other aspects of
dealing with the message. To illustrate this they had designed a
banner expressive of their intent. As I remember, it showed two
hands reaching down from the clouds and two hands reaching up
from a human being on earth, and the inscription was: Pass on what
you have received. A questioner asked me my opinion of the banner; and I said that I thought it admirable, but I would want another
banner to hang alongside it, a banner with the inscription: Before
you pass it on, however, make your own contribution. The necessity of each generation making its contribution to the development
of the understanding of Jesus should be emphasized. Jesus had a
parable that featured a man who was very happy to pass on what he
had received; he wrapped up the money given to him by the master
in a handkerchief and buried it lest any of it be lost. The judgment
on that man is well known; he was regarded as a worthless servant
because he had not added to what he had received. The addition to
and development of the Jesus tradition in the stages of the formation of the Gospels are in my mind parabolic of an essential Christian duty in proclaiming Jesus.

**Q. 44. But does not such an approach to the Gospels, involving
developing tradition, mean that basically they are not any more to
be considered as historical?**

No, I would insist that they are historical in the sense that they
stem from and have as their basic content the tradition of what
Jesus did and said in his lifetime. They are not *literal* accounts of
what he did and said, however, even if they are historical. They are
not accounts such as would be supplied today by tape recorders or
reporters taking notes and transcribing those notes for publication
the next day.

Interestingly, it was precisely under the title of "the historical truth of the Gospels" that the Roman Pontifical Biblical Commission in 1964 expounded this approach. At the end of the discussion of the three stages of development (Q. 40), the Commission commented on the relationship between history and such a developing tradition by stating that the truth of the story is not affected by the fact that the evangelists relate the words and deeds of the Lord in a different order and do not express his sayings literally, even though they preserve the sense of the sayings. The reason why the truth is not affected is because the doctrine and life of Jesus were not reported simply for the purpose of being remembered, but were preached so as to offer the church a basis of faith and moral practice. Let me summarize all that I have been saying: This proclamation of Gospel material flowing from the ministry of Jesus does not have a biographical intent and does not bring about literal preservation; it has as its goal adaptation to the needs of the living audiences, and within that framework it may be called historical.

Q. 45. All that sounds nice, but it is too general. Amidst such development, can we be certain of the exact words that Jesus spoke in his lifetime?

We can be certain of the words that Mark, Matthew, Luke, and John wrote. That is what the Holy Spirit inspired and what God has given us. When we try to go back beyond those written Gospels to reconstruct earlier stages, we are exercising a perfectly understandable modern curiosity; but we must recognize that God in His providence did not give us such earlier stages. Thus reconstructions will always suffer from the limitations of our scholarly tools.

In some instances, by looking at a statement and its variations in two, three, or four Gospels, we can attain high plausibility as to the form in which Jesus spoke this statement; and we can ascertain in which tradition developments came by way of explication. Other times we cannot attain such plausibility and we simply have to settle for two diverse forms of the same statement of Jesus. It is not impossible, of course, that Jesus said something similar in two different ways; but we should not resort to that as a normal explanation. The normal explanation will be that in thirty to fifty years of oral proclamation the same saying has undergone variation. If you look at your own experience, you will realize that such developments are to be expected in oral recounting.

Yet let me make two positive observations lest you be disappointed by the answer pointing to limitations that I just gave—limitations not to be blamed on biblical scholars, for we are not the ones who wrote the Gospels. The differences and variations in the reported sayings of Jesus are objectively before us in the four Gospels; all that biblical scholars are trying to do is to explain discrepancies that have been there for some nineteen hundred years. The first observation on the positive side of this situation is that variations that we find in the Gospel reporting of a given saying show the multivalent value of the teaching. It has been developed in different ways precisely because inherently it contained the possibility of being applied to different situations with different nuances. I compare the variations in the four Gospels to the situation of having a very large diamond or precious gem on display in the room of a museum. The diamond is on a stand in the center encased in glass, lighted from all sides; when one enters one can see one side of it and admire the beauty, but it is only by walking around all four sides that one sees the whole of the stone and all the beauty. The variations that the evangelists have preserved, or even have themselves promoted, are differing insights into the same teaching of Jesus.

The second positive observation calls us to remember that when Jesus spoke, many did not understand him and did not believe. If one had an exact tape recording of his words, one would have a message that often was not comprehended. What we have in the developed tradition, presented in the four Gospels, is a message that stems from faith and is adapted to produce faith in a comprehending audience. This may help to explain why in God's providence the Holy Spirit did not inspire a verbatim literal account of the words and deeds of Jesus but a distillation from a developing tradition. Repetition would not necessarily produce faith. The evangelistic task which involves preserving, adapting, explicating, and reordering is part of what makes the Gospels "Good News."

Q. 46. Let me press you. Can you give us any idea of what percentage of Jesus' words reported in the Gospels has remained the same and what percentage is different?

Frankly, I cannot. And if I attempted an answer I would have to warn you that very different answers would be given by other scholars. A lot depends on the criteria used for determining authenticity; and I find that some scholars, in their desire to be absolutely accurate, are minimalistic in their approach to authenticity. I tend to be more conservative on that issue; and my attitude is that specific developments beyond Jesus' authentic words have to be proved or shown plausible, but not simply assumed. More radical scholars would start at the other end and argue that one must assume church *creation* unless one can prove derivation from Jesus. Yet is it logical that those who proclaimed Jesus were not really interested in what he had said, but only in their own creative perceptions of meaning that they could relate to him? The whole thrust of that Roman Pontifical Biblical Commission statement on "The Historical Truth of the Gospels" (Q. 40 above) is to stress a substantial continuity from Jesus to the Gospels, and I favor that.

Q. 47. The questions so far and your answers have been dealing with what Jesus said. I think there is a bigger problem about what Jesus did. How authentic are the miracles of Jesus?

In some responses, especially from the more radical movements in modern biblical scholarship, another factor enters into dealing with the miracles. No one doubts that people can speak, but some in the modern world doubt the existence of miracles. (I am not going to enter into the definition of a miracle here, as to whether it defies all laws of nature, etc.; I do not want to take refuge in the niceties of language. We all know what the issue is: the healing of the sick, the resuscitation of the dead, the stilling of storms, etc.) The famous German scholar Rudolf Bultmann categorized the Gospel miracles as nonhistorical on the general philosophical principle that modern people do not believe in miracles. I refuse, as do

many others, to let such a philosophical answer govern the historical issue. A modern philosophical understanding of reality is not to
be assumed as one-hundred-percent correct and normative for what
might have been. Nor is it really certain that modern people do not
believe in miracles. Despite the put-down that those who do are not
modern, I suspect that if one counted heads, more would believe in
the miraculous than disbelieve.

Miracles must be dealt with, in my judgment, in the same way
as the sayings of Jesus. If one goes behind the Gospels (and the
evangelists surely believed that Jesus did miraculous things) to earlier tradition, one finds the evidence for Jesus as healer to be as old
as the evidence for him as speaker of parables. Thus in terms of the
antiquity of Christian tradition I find no reason to dismiss the
miraculous from the ministry of Jesus. Indeed, one of the oldest
memories of him may have been that he did wondrous things—a
memory that could have circulated not only among believers but
among nonbelievers. The Jewish historian Josephus has a famous
passage on Jesus, at least part of which seems to be authentic. In the
90s he wrote (*Antiquities* 18.3.3; #63); "He was a doer of wonderful
deeds, a teacher of people who receive the truth with pleasure." To
my mind both those elements, doer and teacher, are part of the
authentic tradition.

**Q. 48. Once more, can we be specific? You are telling us that in
your view the general tradition of Jesus' miracles is a genuine historical reminiscence—Jesus did wonderful things by way of healing,
etc.—but can we know in the case of an individual miracle that
Jesus did it?**

Once again, when one seeks to go beyond the Gospel accounts
to a pre-Gospel stage, one must weigh the evidence. Are you speaking about a miracle that is preserved in all the Gospel traditions,
e.g., the multiplication of the loaves, or are you speaking of a miracle that is preserved in only one Gospel? If the answer is only one
Gospel, that does not mean that it was invented by either the evangelist or his tradition; but it does allow greater possibility that this
miracle story flowed from a later understanding about Jesus. When

diverse traditions have the same miracle, obviously the evidence for that miracle is of an earlier date.

Let me give an example so that you will see the problems we are faced with. In Mark 11:14 we hear that Jesus cursed a fig tree; in 11:20–21 we hear that on the next day the disciples saw that the fig tree had withered. In Matt 21:19 we are told that when Jesus cursed the fig tree, it withered immediately. Which of those two reports do you think is likely to contain the older, less-developed tradition? Most scholars would immediately choose Mark's account because comparable situations show that Matthew has a habit of making the miracles more dramatic and intense. When one turns to Luke, one finds that Luke has no such cursing of a fig tree, but in 13:6–9 has a *parable* about the fig tree wherein a man who in vain seeks fruit from one wants to cut it down. The vinedresser tells him to wait a year until it is fertilized and cared for and only then, if it bears no fruit, to cut it down. Are these echoes of the same event in the life of Jesus? If so, which is likely to be the more original: the miracle of cursing the fig tree and having it wither, or the parable about an intent to cut down the tree unless it bears fruit? Some who distrust the miraculous would immediately opt for the Lucan parable as more original. Others who recognize Luke's tendency to soften anything reflective of Jesus' anger might think rather that an angry action of Jesus has been translated into a parabolic reflection. This is what I mean by studying each miracle story for its own value and judging the tradition or traditions that report it and the tendency of those traditions before one makes a judgment on the historicity of the individual miracle. The solid contention that a miracle tradition about Jesus is authentic does not require that one accept the literal historicity of every Gospel miracle.

Yet, I warn very strongly against a modernization of the miracles in a liberal fashion, e.g., explaining the multiplication of the loaves in terms of Jesus touching the hearts of those present so that they opened their knapsacks and brought out hidden food. That is absolute nonsense: it is not what the Gospels narrate, but rather an attempt to evade the import of what is narrated. Another example is to explain his walking on the water in terms of shallow depth. The explanation is shallow, not the water.

Q. 49. I see a difference between the words and the miracles of Jesus. His words have enduring value, but what value is it to us to know that the healings of Jesus are historical? We normally cannot heal that way today.

I do not want to get into the issue of miraculous healings today. Of course, many miracles are cited for the canonization of saints, and I accept the seriousness of the investigations of such phenomena. The real issue is larger, namely, that even if miracles do occur today, they are not part of our normal ways of healing. Therefore, the issue remains of how a ministry of Jesus filled with miraculous healings is of help to us in our relationship with God and our understanding of human need.

Here I think we can be quite positive, providing we analyze correctly what is at stake in two different worldviews. If we encounter a young boy who suddenly falls down and begins to thrash about and froth at the mouth, despite our lack of medical knowledge, we might immediately suspect a seizure of epilepsy and bring the boy to a doctor who, if he analyzes the sickness as epilepsy, will apply a medical treatment. We would not dream of driving out a demon from this boy; yet that is precisely what Jesus does in Mark 9:14–27. I for one do not think that Jesus possessed modern scientific knowledge or that a modern doctor, were he somehow transported back into antiquity, would have to judge that this was a case of demon possession rather than of epilepsy. These are two different worldviews, one of which involves science, the other of which looks at the issues theologically. The answer is not that modern medicine is wrong, or that we must believe that *all* cases of demon possession (including the possession of houses and pigs) in the Gospels are to be accepted as factual historical accounts.

Working within the worldview of his time, Jesus, by driving out demons in his process of healing, is indicating that sickness is not simply a bodily ailment but is a manifestation of the power of evil in the world. I do not see why even the most modern of Christians should have a problem with that. If we believe that when God accomplishes His plan, not only will there be "salvation of souls" but a blessing extended on the whole universe, so that what was destructive will end and there will be no more suffering and tears

and disasters and death, then we should recognize that such suffer-
ings, tears, disasters and death are representative of alienation from
God and of evil. I do not mean that the person subject to them is
evil or has committed evil, but that the very existence of such
factors indicates the incompleteness of God's plan. By treating not
only diseases but also natural disasters like storms as opposed to the
kingdom (or rule) of God, Jesus is dramatizing a basic biblical
understanding of God and the world.

Modern medicine has come to recognize much more that the
diagnosis of illness in scientific terms does not really take away
issues of good and evil and responsibility. If a doctor analyzes that a
young mother with several children has incurable carcinoma and
will soon die, the anguish that wells up in that mother's heart and
the feelings of the family are not going to be directed against the
carcinoma. If a reproachful question is asked, it will be "Why has
God done this to us?" Increasingly doctors are realizing that the
total treatment of a patient, therefore, has to bring in counseling
and religious support beyond medical analysis. If a huge hurricane
destroys a man's home and family, he is not going to get angry at a
high pressure/low pressure situation; he is going to ask about God's
providence. To this day people continue to relate sickness, disaster,
and death to good and evil, rather than simply to scientific causes. A
Jesus who proclaimed both in word and in deed that the coming of
God's kingdom meant an end to such evil as sickness, disaster, and
death has a relevance and a message in a modern world where we
may know better the scientific factors that enter in to such catastrophes, but we are perhaps more impoverished in dealing with
their psychological and spiritual aspects.

What I have just been saying is another way of looking at the
issue that I emphasized in a previous response (Q. 40) when I spoke
about Stage One of Gospel formation. Jesus deals with this issue as
a Jew of the first third of the first century; yet he gives God's answer
to the question. Our response should not consist in trying to accept
the Jewish outlook of the first third of the first century (which
psychologically we can scarcely recapture, and historically would
distort), but in seeing what Jesus was proclaiming and in translating
that into the language of people of the twentieth, and soon the
twenty-first, century.

Q. 50. Are you then saying there were no demon possessions, or there are none today?

Of course not. What right would I have to pretend to know the limitations of the mystery of evil? I am recognizing, as I think most modern scholars would, that one cannot deal easily with the historicity of the individual stories of demon possession in the New Testament. For instance, it is noteworthy that John's Gospel narrates no demonic possessions. Yet I am also insisting that there is a deeper message behind those stories, and that should not be obscured if a judgment is passed that some of the demon stories reflect another worldview.

You are *free* not to accept as historical the situation implied in the parabolic saying of Jesus about a demon who goes out from a person and wanders through desert places seeking rest (Luke 11:24) —that is not far from the notion of haunted country houses. But if you choose to believe that in Jesus' time demons actually did dwell in such places, you have no right to force that belief on others in the name of Gospel inerrancy. Similarly, with demons leaving a possessed man and invading a herd of pigs (Mark 5:12). One must allow for a different first-century worldview shared by Jesus and the evangelists. Yet, if you are among those who do not think that such details are historical, you are not free to dismiss the religious import of the narratives. Such dismissal of significance is not a mark of sophistication but of superficiality.

Q. 51. Do you believe in a devil?

I never understand why my personal belief is a matter of great importance to large audiences even though I am not reticent about it. In fact, the direct answer to your question is yes.

But I suspect that what you want pertains more to the *evidence* for the existence of a devil, and in particular the biblical evidence. Whatever may have been popular belief in pre-exilic times—the period before the Babylonian exile of 587–539 B.C.—the biblical material written before that period does not give much indication of belief in a devil in the normal sense of the word. The tempter dramatized as a serpent in Genesis is not called a devil (although that does happen later in the Book of Revelation 12:9); and the Satan of the Book of Job is more a heavenly prefect of discipline than a principle of evil. After the exilic period and surely with the admixture of a good deal of Persian influence, Judaism does manifest belief in both a principal force of evil (devil, Satan, Belial, etc.) and in hordes of demons, some of whom possess people. Clearly the New Testament writers shared the view of the Judaism of their time on the reality of the demonic; and subsequent Christian theology, until our own time, has regarded that belief as serious and normative.

I remain curious about people who state with certitude that there is no devil, since I do not know how they know this; and a universal negative is most difficult to prove. As for people who believe in the existence of a supreme intelligent principle of good, namely God, I am not at all clear as to why they would feel impelled to deny the existence of a supreme (under God) intelligent principle of evil. Does the recent history of the world incline one to doubt the existence of such an evil force at work? Indeed, to the more pessimistic, the recent history of the world might make it easier to believe in the devil than to believe in God.

As for church doctrine, it is my understanding (although I always insist that I do not claim to be an expert in systematic theology) that the existence of the devil is normally considered part of infallibly taught Catholic doctrine. That is a very modest doctrine; it does not insist on describing the devil or specifying plurality, or any of the other aspects that so many imagine in their picture of the devil. I would argue that it is almost impossible to understand Jesus' proclamation in word and deed of the coming of the kingdom of God without understanding at the same time the opposition that stems from a kingdom of evil already established in this world. Moreover, I do not find much in our modern experience of the continued proclamation of God's kingdom to make me think that deliberate resistance by evil is something that belongs solely to the worldview of the first century. That is something quite different from attributing almost every sickness to a demon.

Q. 52. You have been questioned about the historicity of many aspects of the Gospel story: Jesus' sayings, his miracles, demons. But what about the crowning event in the Gospel story? I have heard that reputable theologians, including Catholics, say that their faith would not be upset if the body of Jesus was discovered in Palestine. Do you as a biblical scholar think it necessary to believe in a physical resurrection?

Your pointed question raises a large issue, but an issue that I do not think we can afford to avoid or treat without precision. I have many times, both verbally and in writing, maintained that the statement of anyone today that "my faith would not be disturbed if they found the body of Jesus in Palestine" is quite irrelevant. We are not asked to believe in the resurrection of Christ upon the authority of any modern theologian. But we are asked to believe in the resurrection upon the authority of the apostolic witnesses. Therefore the question must be: Would the faith of Peter or Paul be disturbed if they found the body of Jesus in Palestine? I maintain that the biblical evidence points to the fact that Peter and Paul preached a risen Jesus whose body had not corrupted in the grave. *There is not an iota of New Testament evidence that any Christian thought the body of Jesus was still in the grave corrupting.* Therefore, I think that the biblical evidence greatly favors the corporeal resurrection of Jesus.

You may note that you asked about the physical resurrection and I responded in terms of bodily resurrection. The question of physical resurrection touches on the nature of the risen body and about that there may be dispute. The basic issue is bodily resurrection. Was the body that was placed in the tomb on Friday raised into glory so that it no longer remained in the tomb or rotting in the earth? And that question I answer affirmatively according to the biblical evidence.

Having been clear on that point, let me add some factors that may clarify why objections are raised or why theologians speak the way they sometimes do about the body of the risen Jesus. In terms of the New Testament evidence, the stories of the finding of the empty tomb narrated in all four Gospels are often designated as late. The reasons for that include the fact that while Paul preaches the risen Jesus, he never narrates the story of the finding of the empty tomb, or mentions the tomb of Jesus. Personally, I do not find that silence very alarming, since Paul mentions practically nothing else about the historical details of the ministry of Jesus. Even today one could preach on the resurrection at length without getting into the matter of the finding of the empty tomb. Another factor that suggests to scholars that the stories are late are the varying details in the narrative: one angel or two angels, standing or sitting, the tomb already opened, or opened by an angel who descends, what the angel says. These variations in the Gospels I would regard as reflecting the oral development of the tradition. But underlying all such variations is a solidly attested tradition by all four Gospels that the tomb was empty on Easter morning. To me the authenticity of that tradition, not the lateness of the varying stories in which it is contained, is the issue. The very fact that Mary Magdalene is remembered in the Gospels (and she is the basic witness to the finding of the tomb) favors the thesis that this was a historical Christian memory. Moreover, as often pointed out, if any Jewish nonbeliever could have gone and pointed to the body of Jesus in a tomb, the Christian proclamation of the resurrection would have been impossible. I see no reason to think then that the emptiness of the tomb of Jesus is not historical.

Of course, I understand that that tomb could have been empty for various reasons. So did the evangelists: In John 20, Mary Magdalene's first suggestion for why the tomb is empty is that someone has taken the body. Matt 28:13–15 reports the existence of a Jewish claim that Jesus' disciples stole the body at night. The emptiness of the tomb does not prove the resurrection; rather the resurrection became the standard explanation of the emptiness of the tomb. The latter fact suggests to me that Christian *proclamation* of the resurrection implied the impossibility of finding Jesus' body and, therefore, implied the corporeal aspect of the resurrection of Jesus.

Another factor that must be taken into account by Roman Catholics is church teaching. In my opinion the bodily resurrection of Jesus represents the teaching of the ordinary magisterium of the church in such a way that it comes under the rubric of infallibly taught doctrine. (I do not claim that this is taught by the extraordinary magisterium of the church exercised in creedal, conciliar, or papal definitions, but that it is part of the general and universal teaching and understanding of the church throughout the ages.) Very responsible systematic theologians have queried this by insisting that the precision *bodily* is not provably part of the infallible teaching. They are entitled to their view; but I do point out that in recent years where the bodily resurrection has been challenged, the reaction of church authority has been swift and definite, so that at least the office of the church that supervises doctrine does not regard a nonbodily resurrection as an alternative to be taught in Catholic circles. Because I judge bodily resurrection to be taught infallibly, I do not hesitate to invoke that as a reason why I believe it—not over against the biblical evidence, but in consonance with the biblical evidence. (I never see the church's authority as a purely extrinsic factor; the church teaches authoritatively on such issues because it has lived with the Bible and proclaimed it over the centuries and has been guided by the Holy Spirit in interpreting the Bible.)

Nevertheless, these two factors that I have mentioned, namely, the theory of some biblical scholars that the empty tomb story is a late development in the New Testament and the disagreement of some scholars about the precision of church teaching, must be kept in mind in understanding why a debate has arisen over the bodily resurrection. One may defensibly maintain, however, that the majority of centrist biblical scholars would recognize that a resurrection of the body is what New Testament writers and preachers are talking about and that a majority of centrist theologians would hold that a bodily resurrection is infallibly taught by the ordinary magisterium of the church. For non-Catholics the latter issue may not be of importance; yet many of them would insist on bodily resurrection as part of the inerrancy of Scripture.

Q. 53. You are clear on the bodily resurrection, but come back to that issue of "physical" resurrection. Why do you avoid that word?

I avoid that word for several biblical reasons. In I Cor 15:42–50, Paul discusses the resurrection of the body. Remember that he had seen the risen Jesus; therefore I suspect that his description of the resurrection of Christians has been influenced by his experience of the resurrection of Jesus. He contends that the risen body will be spiritual not *psychikos,* which many translate as "physical." Whether or not that is the best translation may be debated, but there is no doubt that Paul maintains that what is sown in the grave is raised with very different properties. There is an enormous transformation of the body so that he can contend that "flesh and blood cannot inherit the kingdom of God" (I Cor 15:50). Paul thinks of bodily resurrection, but the transformation indicated by his words seems to take the risen body out of the realm of the physical into the spiritual. Similarly, while the Gospel passages clearly describe the appearance of the risen Jesus as a bodily appearance, they attribute to him properties that are not the properties of the physical body as we know it, e.g., the ability to move through a closed door, to move from one place to another with incredible rapidity, and to appear suddenly.

Let me go on to anticipate an objection. There is one New Testament author who does ascribe physical properties to the risen body, namely, Luke in 24:41–42 where he has Jesus eat. (This goes beyond the identity statements that the risen body of Jesus possessed the marks of the cross, statements found not only in Luke but in John.) Could the risen Jesus eat? It is interesting that just before these verses Luke 24:39 speaks of the flesh and bones of the risen Jesus, while Paul states that the risen body is not flesh and blood, but spiritual. Which view is correct if we are right in seeing an important difference between the two views? Paul saw the risen Jesus; there is no claim that Luke did. In order to stress the corporality of the risen Jesus (which, I have already stated, is accepted by various biblical writers) has Luke dramatized its physicality? Like many other scholars, I am inclined to favor the Pauline position and to think that Luke's vivid narration really means no more than a stress on the true corporality. So far as I can see, the properties of the risen body are an open question; and I would think that holds true even in the teaching of the Catholic Church. While I judge that the church has taught infallibly the bodily resurrection, I find no evidence that it has taught infallibly specific details about the properties of the risen body of Jesus and its physicality. Therefore I suggest avoiding the term physical and using the term bodily. That latter term is closer, in any case, to the real issue.

All this can be expressed in an insistence on two factors in the resurrection: continuity and transformation. The continuity is such that the body of Jesus that was buried in the grave has truly been raised. The transformation is such that the risen body is almost indescribably different from the physical body that walked this earth. Thus when one speaks of "the bodily resurrection," opponents of that view should not be allowed to deride it as if automatically it implied a crassly physical understanding, even to the point of an ability to televise the resurrection to a mass audience. Paul in speaking of a bodily resurrection was much more subtle, and so should we be.

Q. 54. In your response to questions about the historicity of Jesus' life, I noticed that you did not speak about his birth. You and others supposedly claim the birth stories are not historical.

Certainly I have never claimed that. I rarely make an absolute negative statement about historicity because such statements are forbiddingly hard to prove. The way I would phrase the issue is that there are reasons for thinking that the birth stories, which are found in the first two chapters of Matthew and the first two chapters of Luke, are not historical in some, or even many details.

Two facts should be kept in mind in relation to that judgment. Roman Catholics sometimes assume that if one queries the historicity of the birth narratives, one is going against church teaching. That is not true. There is no official church statement in force that the birth narratives are literally historical. Indeed the statement of the Roman Pontifical Biblical Commission on "The Historical Truth of the Gospels" (Q. 40 above) very clearly concerned what the disciples heard and saw of Jesus *during his public ministry* and did not treat the stories of his birth. Afterwards, there was an attempt to have the Commission issue a statement on the historicity of the birth narratives; but it was abandoned in the late 1960s, presumably because such a statement would have been too complicated and perhaps have had to be too nuanced.

The second factor involves why we have a tradition about what Jesus did and said. It is because people who had been with him were in a position to report those sayings and deeds, namely, the disciples and in particular the Twelve. But none of those disciples was present at the birth of Jesus, and so we cannot claim that we have apostolic witness to the birth events.

Q. 55. But do we not have the witness of Mary and Joseph for what happened at the birth?

Perhaps, but that is never claimed in the New Testament. So far as we know, since Joseph never appears in the story of Jesus' ministry, he was dead by the time Jesus was baptized by John. Mary was still alive during the public ministry, but she is never described as accompanying Jesus in his preaching and healing travels. We do not know what relationship Mary had to the apostolic preachers who preserved the tradition. Some imagine Mary recounting to them the stories of the birth; but there is no suggestion of that in the New Testament and, indeed, in the earliest centuries. The real challenge to the notion that the birth stories are simply Mary's reminiscences is that the two stories in Matthew and Luke are so totally different that it is very hard to imagine them coming from the same person. More romantic scholars have occasionally suggested that Joseph was the source of the story in Matthew and Mary the source of the story in Luke; but the hardheaded response, with a touch of humor, is that evidently then Mary and Joseph never spoke to each other, because they had such totally different reminiscences of the same happenings.

Q. 56. What do you regard as crucial differences between the two Gospel birth stories?

In Matthew's story Joseph and Mary live in Bethlehem and have a house there (2:11). They stay in Bethlehem until the child is nearly two years old (2:16) and the only reason they cannot go back after the flight to Egypt is their fear of Herod's son. Consequently they go to a city called Nazareth with the clear implication that they have not been there before (2:22–23). In Luke, Mary and Joseph live in Nazareth and go to Bethlehem only because of the census

(1:26; 2:4). After the birth of the child, having stopped in Jerusalem on the way, they go quickly back to Nazareth and there they remain (2:39). There is no reference in Luke to the family being in Bethlehem for almost two years after the birth, to the coming of the magi to Jerusalem and to Bethlehem with all the éclat that must have produced, no reference to the killing of children in Bethlehem or to the flight into Egypt. Indeed, in his narrative of peaceful return from Bethlehem through Jerusalem to Nazareth, Luke would have no room for such horrendous events and such a detour into Egypt. In Matthew's account there is no reference to a census and the whole atmosphere of the story is different from Luke's.

What we should recognize is that each story in its own way relates factors that are functionally equivalent. For instance, Matthew tells of an annunciation to Joseph, while Luke tells of an annunciation to Mary; and each annunciation has the function of identifying the child to be born as the Messiah and as "God-With-Us" or the Son of God. Matthew tells of magi who come after the birth of Jesus to adore him, while Luke tells of shepherds who come after the birth to adore the child; each scene has the function of showing that God's revelation in Jesus will be responded to by belief and praise, on the part of Gentiles in Matthew and on the part of Jews in Luke.

Q. 57. If the two birth accounts are so different, why cannot we suppose that one account is historical and the other symbolic? Why are doubts raised about the historicity of each?

Some scholars do respond to the differences among the birth narratives by choosing the very route you suggest. Particularly among Roman Catholic scholars, the choice for a historical account favors Luke. Mary is the main subject in Luke, and the guess is made that she was the source of that story. I do not think the solution can be so simple because the criteria of historicity raise problems about events described by Luke as well as events described by Matthew.

Let me give you some examples. Both Matthew and Luke describe events that certainly should have left a record in the public arena. Matthew describes an unusual astronomical phenomenon: a star that rose in the East, seemingly led the magi to Jerusalem, then reappeared and came to rest over the birthplace of Jesus in Bethlehem (2:2, 9). In my *Birth of the Messiah* I examined every suggestion made from the astronomical records of the period of Jesus' birth: comets, conjunction of planets, and supernova stars. It was apparent that no astronomical record exists of what is described in Matthew (despite occasional journalistic headlines to the contrary).

In the case of Luke's census by Caesar Augustus of the whole world when Quirinius was governor of Syria (2:1–2), a census that presumably was made when Herod the Great was King of Judea (1:5), we have a similar problem. In the same *Birth of the Messiah,* I examined all the historical records about the governorship of Quirinius in Syria and censuses by Augustus. There never was a single census that covered the whole world under Augustus, and the census (of Judea, not involving Nazareth!) that took place under Quirinius occurred about ten years after the death of Herod the Great, and presumably, therefore, after the birth of Jesus. One is hard-pressed, then, to think that either evangelist is accurate on public events. Probably postfactum (after the resurrection) the birth of Jesus was associated with loose memories of phenomena that occurred in a period ten years before or after his birth.

Let me make an application of another criterion of historicity. One would expect what is narrated in the infancy narrative to agree with what is narrated in the body of the Gospel. According to Matt 2, when the magi came to Herod the Great, and he and the chief priests and the scribes learned about the birth of the King of the Jews, all Jerusalem was disturbed by the event. Yet when Jesus appears in the public ministry nobody seems to know much about him or to expect anything of him (Matt 13:54–56). In particular, Herod's son, Herod Antipas, knows nothing about Jesus (Luke 9:7–9). According to Luke, Elizabeth the mother of John the Baptist was a relative of Mary the mother of Jesus and so the two children were related. Yet in the public ministry there is never a suggestion that John the Baptist is a relative of Jesus; and in John 1:33 the Baptist says specifically, "I did not know him."

This is not an exhaustive list of problems that raise doubts about the historicity of the infancy narrative, e.g., the genealogy of

Jesus in Matthew does not agree with the genealogy of Jesus in Luke, and neither one is free of major difficulties. Thus one is not being wantonly skeptical in judging that it is not so easy to classify one narrative as historical and the other as symbolic. In particular, in reference to the thesis that Luke gives Mary's reminiscences of the events, one has not only the general problem of historicity (the census issue just discussed) but the seemingly inaccurate description of the customs and behavior of Mary when she brings the child to Jerusalem. In 2:22 and following, the Jewish laws of the presentation of the firstborn and the purification of the mother are confusedly described and a wrong supposition seems to be made that more than Mary needed purification ("their purification"). This does not give the appearance of accurate family reminiscence.

Q. 58. Well, if the birth stories are not historical, what value do they have? Are they any better than folkloric tales?

Forgive me for rather bluntly insisting that you pay attention to what I said. *I did not say* that the birth stories are not historical. I gave reasons why scholars think that some of the events described in those stories may not be historical. I think there are historical details in the birth narratives, although neither Matthew's nor Luke's narrative is completely historical.

I always emphasize that, besides disagreeing on certain matters, the two evangelists also agree on what might be called the most important points. Both have an annunciation of the future greatness of the child, before the child's birth. That means they both agree on a providential divine preparation and, indeed, on a revelation. Both agree that the child was conceived without a human father—the astounding claim for the virginal conception. Both agree that the child was of the House of David through the Davidic heritage of Joseph, and both agree that the birth took place in the city of Bethlehem. Both agree that ultimately the family went to settle in Nazareth. These are very important agreements, and I would argue that a case can be made for the historicity of such details.

Yet I also argue that too myopic a concern with historicity can blind people to the great value that the stories have in themselves. Matthew's infancy narrative is a carefully done "catechism" of the basic message of the Scriptures of Israel, i.e., what we would call the Old Testament. In the genealogy we have the stories of the patriarchs and the kings recalled simply by the mention of the names, so that we are reminded that Jesus is heir of the virtues associated with Abraham, Isaac, Jacob, David, Solomon, etc. In a sermon that I am very fond of (reprinted in *A Coming Christ in Advent* [Liturgical Press, 1988], pp. 16–26), I have stressed the significance of having even unknown names, such as we find in the last section of Matthew's genealogy, as part of the message concerning a Messiah who will preach to those who would not be considered important by the world's standards. I have pointed out the prophetic passages in Matthew's infancy narrative as an attempt to include in the message of Jesus' birth the testimony of Isaiah, Jeremiah, Hosea, etc. The Matthean Joseph story, with its dreams and journey to Egypt, evokes the Old Testament narrative of Joseph, even as the appearance of the wicked King Herod who slays children evokes the memory of the Pharaoh in Egypt who tried to destroy Moses. In short, what Matthew is doing is retelling the story of Israel because it is an essential introduction to the Gospel proper which begins with the baptism of Jesus by John the Baptist.

I find a similar message in the Lucan infancy narrative, done with even more exquisite artistic balancing of details. There is a parallel between the annunciation of the Baptist's birth and the annunciation of Jesus' birth culminating in the coming together of the two mothers. This is followed by another parallel between the birth and circumcision of the Baptist, hailed by a canticle, and the birth, circumcision, and presentation of Jesus, hailed by a canticle. The Old Testament motifs in Luke are even more subtle than in Matt, e.g., only if one knows the Bible will one recognize that the situation of Zechariah and Elizabeth is exactly like that of Abraham and Sarah (too aged and too barren to have a child). In Luke 1:18, Zechariah speaks the same words as Abraham speaks in Gen 15:8. The presentation of Jesus in the Temple before the aged Simeon strongly resembles the presentation of Samuel in the Temple before the aged Eli, even as the canticle of Mary (the Magnificat) strongly resembles the canticle of Samuel's mother Hannah (I Sam 2:1–10).

Thus by a type of superimposition both evangelists are telling us of Old Testament scenes and characters who are preparations for Jesus.

I would also point out that each infancy narrative is an anticipation of the Gospel and its proclamation. In each the basic message enunciated by an angel is that Jesus is God's Son, thus the christological identity of the Messiah. In each that message is received with obedience, by Joseph in Matthew and by Mary in Luke. In each, others come and adore (magi in Matthew, shepherds in Luke) as a sign that the gospel will be received. In each there is also a rejection (by Herod, the chief priests, and the scribes in Matthew; and implied in the warning in Luke 2:34: "This child is set for *the fall* and rise of many in Israel."). The infancy narratives are properly treated only when we emphasize the content, namely, the Old Testament background and the basic christological identity of Jesus, including the fact that his coming forces decision, self-judgment, and (on the part of some) even hostility. The modern approach, therefore, avoids both the fairy-tale element that was raised in the question as well as an oversentimentalized baby imagery.

Q. 59. In your answer you mentioned an angelic message to Joseph and Mary. How seriously should we take the angelic? Are there angels?

Previous questioners showed interest in the demonic and the devil (Q. 50–51 above), so I guess it is only fair that the angels should get their share of attention. Just as with devils, so also with angels one must distinguish the evidence in Israelite thought before the Babylonian exile (587–539 B.C.) and post-exilic thought. While in early Israelite thought God is conceived as having a heavenly court, surrounded by those beings called the "sons of God," who would be similar to angels, the most important stress is on "the angel of the Lord." This is not a truly separate being but an earthly and, generally, visible representation of God's own presence. Thus in the great encounter between Moses and God on Mount Sinai (Horeb) in Exodus 3, we hear first of the angel of the Lord appearing to Moses in the flaming bush but then very quickly the Lord is there and speaks. After the exile there is a development in Jewish angelic thought where the angels truly become distinct beings and are even given names. In the Old Testament Michael, Raphael, and Gabriel are named.

It is interesting to see the echo of this history in the two Gospel infancy narratives. In Matthew it is the angel of the Lord who appears in a dream to Joseph on plural occasions and conveys God's message to him. Matthew is using Old Testament language for divine revelation, even if, we may suspect, Matthew by this time thinks of a real angel rather than simply using the angel of the Lord to describe God's presence. Luke, on the other hand, gives us the named angel Gabriel as the divine messenger; and there can be no doubt that Luke thinks of an individual angel. Since Gabriel is the revealing angel in the Book of Daniel who explains the great vision of the end times, his presence in Luke's infancy narrative is a signal that what Daniel had prophesied is now coming true—the end time is at hand in the conception and birth of Jesus.

You asked me whether there really are angels, and my response would be similar to the one I gave to the question of whether there really are devils. In brief, there is no way to prove there are not; Jesus and the New Testament authors clearly thought there were and that has been the church view ever since; it is commonly thought that the church has in her infallible teaching taught the existence of angels and their guardian function; and in the ladder of being, stretching from the all-powerful God to His most insignificant creation, the angels can plausibly find a place between God and human beings. Thus I find very good reasons for believing that there are angels and practically no reason for denying their existence.

Q. 60. In all your references to the beginning of Matthew and Luke you have spoken of infancy or birth stories. Yet there is in Luke a story of Jesus at age twelve. What do we know of Jesus' youth?

Frankly, very little. I do not wish to get into the complicated analysis of that story in Luke, but if one examines it very carefully it is almost independent of all that precedes. Mary's reaction to what

Jesus says and her puzzlement is hard to understand after all that has been revealed to her previously, but would be very easy to understand if the story of Jesus at age twelve was once independent.

Lest, however, I confuse you with too much information, let me concentrate on the function of the Lucan story. In the first chapter of Luke *an angel* tells Mary and the reader that Jesus is God's Son. In the third chapter of Luke *the voice of God* at the baptism tells the reader that Jesus is God's Son. In the second chapter, precisely in this story of Jesus at age twelve, the first time that he speaks in the Gospel, *Jesus himself* identifies God as his Father: "Did you not know that I would be in my Father's house?" Therefore the function is christological: the Jesus of the ministry who speaks and acts as God's Son already spoke and acted as God's Son from the first time he appeared on the scene.

Similarly, in apocryphal gospels concerning Jesus' youth, there is a retrojection of acts of power and statements from the ministry reflecting self-awareness. Consistently, the underlying desire is to show continuity throughout Jesus' life. Already in the bosom of his family he had the same knowledge and power that he manifested in the ministry. Indeed, he even encountered some of the same opposition. You may have heard of a story from the *Infancy Gospel of Thomas* of how Jesus as a boy made clay birds and they flew away. What is often not remembered from that story is that a certain Jew who saw it complained to Joseph that Jesus was working with clay on the Sabbath—the same type of protest registered against Jesus during his public ministry. Thus the function of the few boyhood stories that we have is theological rather than primarily historical.

Q. 61. In the stories about Jesus' birth and boyhood Mary plays a role. How important is Mary biblically?

One would have to answer that by making a distinction among the Gospels. Mary is mentioned in all four Gospels and at the beginning of the Book of Acts. In what most scholars consider to be the earliest Gospel, namely, MARK, Mary only makes one appearance during the ministry of Jesus. In 3:31–35, and thus early in the Marcan story, she and the brothers of Jesus come looking for him, seemingly to bring him back home since they are puzzled at the intensity of his new style of life and preaching (see 3:21). Their appearance causes Jesus to ask his disciples the question of who constitute his family—namely, his family in relation to the work of proclaiming God's kingdom. Jesus is very definite that in this context anyone who does the will of God is brother and sister and mother to him: In other words, not automatically the natural family by birth, but a family constituted by discipleship. That is one of the most fundamental issues connected with references to Jesus' mother (and brothers) in the New Testament.

In MATTHEW, the Marcan scene is repeated; but Matthew's overall picture of Mary is softened by his indication in chapter 1 that Mary conceived Jesus not by a human father but by the Holy Spirit. Therefore without doubt Matthew presents the reader with a positive view of Mary, even if that picture is never worked out in the pages of the ministry in any great detail.

In LUKE there is an enormous expansion of the role of Mary. Whereas she is only a background figure in the Matthean infancy story, in the Lucan story she is a main actor. And Luke solves the tension between a family constituted by discipleship and the natural family of Jesus by birth. He does this in the account of the annunciation where Mary hears the word of God from an angel and says "Be it done unto me according to your word" (Luke 1:38). Thus if a disciple is one who hears the word of God and does it, Mary becomes the first Christian disciple because she is the first one to hear the word of God and to consent wholeheartedly that it be done. Indeed Luke goes further by having her then begin already to proclaim the good news in the Magnificat (1:46–55). Luke makes it clear that Mary has been specially favored by God and is blessed among women. In 2:19, 51 we are told that in regard to God's mysterious plan in her Son, she keeps all of these things in her heart—a description that prepares us for a further role of Mary in Jesus' subsequent life. While Luke preserves the basic Marcan scene of the mother and brothers coming and searching for Jesus, he removes from it all contrast between the natural family and a family of disciples (9:19–21). This removal of contrast is consonant with the view that Luke considers the natural family already to be disciples. It also explains why at the beginning of the Book of Acts he includes Mary and the brothers of Jesus, alongside the Twelve and the women, in the group that are gathered in Jerusalem waiting for the Pentecostal outpouring of the Spirit. From beginning to end in the Lucan account Mary is an obedient disciple.

JOHN's treatment, while containing material different from that of Luke, has some of the same tone. In John the mother of Jesus appears in two scenes. At the beginning of the ministry at Cana, her request to Jesus, implicit in the report that the hosts had no more wine, is met at first by a rejection or refusal that reminds the reader that Jesus' action is to be controlled not by family need but by the hour commanded by the Father ("My hour has not yet come": 2:4). Yet when the mother of Jesus shows herself at Jesus' disposition ("Do whatever he tells you"), then Jesus does perform the sign of changing water to wine, a sign that functions within the task given him by the Father of bringing the new divine dispensation into the world. The second scene in which the mother of Jesus appears is at the foot of the cross. Only John reports the presence of friends of Jesus at the foot of the cross, and indeed he concentrates on the two figures whose names he never gives, namely, the disciple whom Jesus loved and the mother of Jesus. These two figures have symbolic importance in the Fourth Gospel. The disciple whom Jesus loved is the ideal disciple who has always remained faithful, even to Jesus on the cross; and this disciple is given to Jesus' mother as her son. Thus the issue of family returns once more. The true family of Jesus left behind by him at the cross and to whom he gives over the Spirit as he dies, is constituted by his mother (the natural family) and the beloved disciple (the family of discipleship), and the two now become one as the disciple becomes Jesus' brother, and Jesus' mother becomes the disciple's own mother.

Thus, even though the Gospel material is limited, the later Gospels make very clear that by the end of the first century a remarkable role in Christian discipleship was being attributed to the mother of Jesus in various parts of the Early Church. In an ecumenical book done by Catholic and Protestant scholars together, *Mary in the New Testament* (New York: Paulist, 1978), we spoke in a language of trajectory. The trajectory of the role of Mary increases in the chronologically later sections of the New Testament and continues in the subsequent church until Mary is proclaimed as the most perfect of all Christians. Perhaps some of our Protestant brothers and sisters might hesitate at the later developments of mariology, but at least this approach through trajectory shows that those later developments are not unrelated to the New Testament.

Q. 62. Among the later developments of mariology that you just mentioned are the Immaculate Conception and the Assumption. Can you relate those to the New Testament?

I do think that those doctrines can be related to the New Testament, but not in a simple way. In my understanding it is not necessary that anyone in the first century would have been able to phrase the idea that Mary was conceived without sin. Nor do I have any way of knowing whether people in the first century would have realized that Mary was taken bodily into heaven (presumably after her death). However, with a trajectory approach, one can show a connection between those clarifications of Mary's privileged state and the role of discipleship that is given to her so clearly in sections of the New Testament.

Let me show this with each doctrine. The doctrine of the Immaculate Conception attributes to Mary a primacy in receiving a privilege that all disciples of Jesus receive. In Christian faith we are delivered through baptism from original sin. (On the biblical status of original sin, see Q. 24.) We Roman Catholics believe that Mary was *conceived* free of original sin—a preparation by God for the sinlessness of Jesus who would take flesh in her womb. If Luke pictures Mary as the first disciple, the Immaculate Conception says that by anticipation the grace of Christ's redemption was given first to Mary even from the time of her conception. She is the first one to receive the fruits of the redemption. The gift of freedom from original sin is a gift to all disciples, but the first Christian disciple has received it first.

As for the Assumption, if it is understood as Mary being taken bodily into heaven after her death, then once again Mary is the first to receive a privilege that will ultimately be given to all Christians.

All believers in Christ will be raised from the dead and taken bodily
to heaven; this deliverance from death is a fruit of the redemption
given to Jesus' disciples. Thus far it has been granted only to Mary,
the first Christian disciple, but eventually it will be granted to all
disciples.

What I have said does not exhaust Mary's privileges or even all
that is associated with the Immaculate Conception and the Assumption; but it places those two doctrines clearly in the trajectory
of discipleship. I think that is helpful ecumenically because it shows
that, even granted the divine bounty to Mary, that bounty is
within the realm of discipleship and redemption by Jesus. To put it
simply, it alleviates Protestant fears that somehow in their esteem of
Mary Catholics are divinizing her. We are recognizing the grace
given by God to the disciples of His Son, of whom Mary is the
premier example. This approach also shows that we are thinking of
Mary in the biblical terms of the especially blessed among women
who has been the first to say, "Be it done unto me according to
your word."

**Q. 63. The privileges of Mary about which you have just spoken
are not mentioned explicitly in the Scriptures. What about the privilege that is mentioned specifically by Matthew and Luke, namely,
the virgin birth?**

Even as with the resurrection (Q. 52 above), I evaluate this as
an important question that has to be handled carefully and in some
detail. Let me begin by saying that I always prefer to speak of the
biblical event as *the virginal conception* rather than as the virgin
birth. What the Scriptures are describing is Mary's conception of
Jesus without a human father. Somewhat later in Christian thought
(the second century) there is an added view that Mary gave birth to
Jesus in a miraculous way that preserved the integrity of her bodily
organs. To avoid confusion with that I want to be precise by speaking of the virginal conception.

Sometimes when people in the audience ask me for my views
concerning the virginal conception, they do so with a certain tense-

ness and even add a clause like "Some people say you don't believe in the virginal conception." Consequently in responding to any question about this biblical event, I like to emphasize that from the very first time that I delivered a major lecture on the subject at the beginning of the 1970s and throughout a good deal of writing on it, including books, my position has been unchanged and clearly stated: I accept the virginal conception, but I do so primarily because of church teaching on that subject. There are many scholars, Protestants and some Roman Catholics, who deny the virginal conception on biblical grounds; I disagree with them, for I contend that the biblical evidence does not contradict the historicity of the virginal conception. Yet I admit that one cannot prove the virginal conception on the basis of biblical evidence, and that is why I would appeal to church doctrine as solving the ambiguities left from the biblical accounts. Having stated that, now let me explain the situation that has produced such division among scholars.

The conception of the child Jesus is mentioned only by Matthew and by Luke; and there is no doubt that for them conception through the Holy Spirit in the womb of the Virgin Mary is meant to have theological import, involving the creative power of God and the uniqueness of the moment in which the Messiah was sent. But beyond that there is also a historical issue: Was the child conceived without the intervention of a human father? Some who deny the historicity of the virginal conception, giving a "no" to that last question, do so because they think that the divine and the miraculous are nonsense. Others who deny the historicity of the virginal conception believe in God and the miraculous but think that in this instance the narrative is purely symbolic: "Born of a virgin" does not mean for them born without a human father, but born with the aid of a divine Father. Particularly in dialogue with the latter group of scholars, I would emphasize that both Matthew and Luke understand and indicate the virginal conception to be factual (as well as theological) and not simply symbolic. Thus, as part of the answer to your question, I would strongly affirm that the two evangelists who wrote about the virginal conception meant it literally, even if they saw in it great theological import. The issue is whether they were correct in their historical judgment.

Q. 64. What kind of evidence can be offered for something so miraculous as a virginal conception?

One type of evidence is theological in nature. Many Christians understand biblical inspiration to mean that whatever the writer thought was inspired by God and inerrant. Consequently, when I say that both Matthew and Luke were thinking of a literal virginal conception, they would respond that then there can be no doubt that such a conception happened, since God guided the evangelists in every message they chose to communicate. In my judgment, Catholics do not share such a simple sense of biblical inerrancy. The Bible teaches faithfully and without error that truth that God intended for the sake of our salvation, says Vatican Council II (*Dogmatic Constitution on Divine Revelation* 3:11). I understand that to mean that in judging inerrancy we cannot simply ask what did the writer intend; we have to ask about the extent to which what the writer communicated is for the sake of our salvation.

For Roman Catholics, therefore, not so much the inerrancy of the Scriptures but church teaching would be a theological factor in judging the historicity of the virginal conception. In creed, council, or papal definition the church has never made a formal statement that the literal historicity of the virginal conception is divinely revealed and must be accepted as a matter of faith. Nevertheless, by its ordinary teaching, which is another guide to what is a matter of faith, I think the church has insisted implicitly on the literal history of the virginal conception. Since as a Roman Catholic, I regard my church's normative teaching based on Scripture to be a special aid in the case where the Scriptures are obscure or nondecisive, I accept the virginal conception.

However, I always warn that there are some Catholic systematic theologians who do not agree with my interpretation of the virginal conception as a church doctrine taught infallibly by the ordinary magisterium; they think I am too conservative on this. Yet, just as with the bodily resurrection (Q. 52 above), in these last twenty years the official teaching organs of the Catholic Church have reacted very sternly against theologians who have publicly denied the historicity of the virginal conception; and that is indicative of the church judgment that this is not merely a symbolic description.

There is another type of evidence that must be considered by all, including those who would accept guidance neither from a theory of scriptural inerrancy nor from church teaching. I refer to the evidence involved in the biblical text itself. Most scholars agree that there is no other reference to the virginal conception of Jesus in the New Testament except Matt 1 and Luke 1. Yet independently of each other these two evangelists do agree on it, despite their setting it in very different contexts—an indicator that it is an idea that antedates both. And so we cannot dismiss it simply as a later invention. In *The Birth of the Messiah* (New York: Doubleday, 1977) I considered the arguments against the historicity of the virginal conception in terms of what could have caused people to create the idea, e.g., by borrowing from pagan stories of the coupling of gods and women, or by meditation on Isaiah 7:14 with its prediction that a young woman would bear a child and call his name Emmanuel (a prophecy that was translated into Greek with emphasis on the virginity of the young woman). I shall not go into those arguments here, but I made a case that none of them explained well the genesis of the idea of a virginal conception. That left the historical explanation as more plausible than any other— more plausible but not proved.

For some that judgment is quite unsatisfactory. They are annoyed that, although not finding the biblical evidence probative, I profess my belief in the virginal conception, allowing the teaching body of the church to guide my judgment. (That position seems to bother both those who deny the virginal conception and those who hold it.) This is no embarrassment to me. If the Bible clearly says one thing, and the church clearly teaches another, to accept both would be schizophrenia. But since both Testaments are the product of believing communities, I see no contradiction in allowing the ongoing life of those communities to serve as an interpretive element, casting light on the obscurities of the biblical record. I would much rather do that than force the biblical evidence, either by insisting that it is totally clear and probative, or by insisting that it disproves when at most it is obscure.

Q. 65. I noticed that in describing Mary's role in the Gospels, you referred to Jesus' mother and "brothers." Isn't that Protestant language?

To discuss the term "brothers," it may help to begin by discussing those who come under that designation, and by far the most famous is a man named James. There are several Jameses in the New Testament. In the lists of the Twelve whom Jesus chose, there is James, the brother of John who is the son of Zebedee, as well as a James "of Alphaeus" (presumably the son of Alphaeus). However, the James at issue here is not a member of the Twelve, but is the one to whom Paul refers to as "the brother of the Lord" (Gal 1:19). Mark 6:3 and Matt 13:55 name him among four "brothers" of Jesus: James, Joses (Joseph), Simon, and Judas (Jude). As leader of the Jerusalem Christians, this James was one of the most important men in the early church. It is to him that the New Testament "Epistle of James" is attributed. I suppose I should mention that by oversimplification later Christians assumed that two of the "brothers," James and Jude, were identical with two of the Twelve Apostles who bore the same names. That is wrong; Acts 1:13–14 keeps quite distinct the Twelve and the "brothers."

Thus several New Testament writers refer to the "brother(s)" of the Lord (Jesus), using the normal Greek word for brother; and the Mark/Matthew reference that I just mentioned speaks subsequently of "sisters" of Jesus. One Catholic translation tried to get around "brothers" by using "brethren," even though that is simply an archaic plural of "brothers," and it was not able to introduce "sistren." We should stick to a literal translation of what the Greek says and not try to bowdlerize it or modify it because it raises questions. And so, to answer your question, "the brothers of Jesus" is not Protestant language but biblical language.

Q. 66. What about Catholic teaching that Mary remained a virgin?

Many times that is described as "Catholic" teaching, but it is more widely held. The Orthodox and Eastern Churches, as well as many "High" Anglicans/Episcopalians, share the view that Mary remained a virgin. While Protestants most often think that the brothers and sisters of Jesus mentioned in the New Testament are Mary's children, and hence that she did not remain a virgin, that was not a major issue at the time of the Reformation. I recall that Luther, Calvin, and Zwingli all used the term "Ever Virgin" (an ancient description of Mary) without objection. Evidently, the modern dispute rose somewhat later from a literalistic reading of the New Testament.

Another distinction is in order. Obviously, if those whom the New Testament calls brothers and sisters of Jesus were blood brothers and sisters, then Mary did not remain a virgin. But if they were not Jesus' blood brothers and sisters, that does not really establish that Mary remained a virgin. The enduring virginity of Mary is something that goes beyond any documentary attestation that we have and represents praise of Mary that stems from our faith. We Roman Catholics consider it a doctrine of the church, but that does not necessarily mean that Mary told anyone that she always remained a virgin. We accept this doctrine of the "Ever Virgin" not on the basis of a biblical text, but from Christian reflection on the sanctity of Mary and the way in which that sanctity was expressed in her life.

Q. 67. I don't understand. You say that in Catholic doctrine Mary remained a virgin, but you also say that the New Testament speaks of the "brothers and sisters" of Jesus. Why does the New Testament call them that?

You are asking a complex question, and so you will have to forgive me if I give a fairly complex answer. While the New Testament uses the language of the "brothers and sisters" of Jesus, it never actually states that these are children of Mary. True, the brothers are frequently associated with Mary (e.g., Mark 3:32; 6:3; John 2:12; Acts 1:14). That association, plus the use of the normal Greek word designating blood brother, might well lead to the conclusion that these were Mary's children if there were no other evidence to the contrary. You may ask yourself whether, if I said I had seen your mother and brothers today, those who heard me would not think I was referring to children your mother had borne.

Nevertheless, by the early second century, as we can see from a story contained in an apocryphal gospel, *The Protevangelium of James* (see Q. 10 above), there was already a tradition circulating that these were not children of Mary. In the elaborate story told in that gospel Joseph is an old man and a widower with children when he marries Mary. Accordingly, when Jesus is born to Mary, the children of Joseph become his brothers and sisters. That is an ingenious solution because it explains not only the designation "brothers and sisters," but also why they are associated with Mary —presumably Joseph died by the time of the public ministry and Mary had raised these children as her own. It also explains how Mary could have remained a virgin even though married to Joseph. We should be honest in acknowledging that *The Protevangelium of James* (notice the author to whom it is attributed: a "brother" of Jesus who should have known the family history) is scarcely a reliable historical source. Nevertheless, it gives evidence of a tradition circulating at a very early period.

Within the New Testament itself there is tenuous evidence that the "brothers" were not blood brothers. In the crucifixion scene in Mark 15:40 and Matt 27:56 there is a reference to one of the women looking on from a distance as "Mary of James and Joses (Joseph)," presumably the mother of James and Joses. These are the names of two of the brothers of Jesus and we may be hearing in this scene that they are children of *another* woman named Mary. (Certainly "of James and Joses" is not a way in which Mark and Matthew would normally refer to Mary, the mother of Jesus.) This information would help to confirm the postbiblical tradition of *The Protevangelium of James* that the "brothers and sisters" were not children of the Virgin Mary.

Why the terminology "brothers and sisters"? I have said that normally the Greek words would refer to uterine or blood brothers and sisters. Yet if there is reason to suspect that these were not blood brothers and sisters (and only under that circumstance), we may resort to the Semitic terminology that could have underlay the Greek. On the one hand, while Greek has terms for "cousins," "step-brothers," "half-brothers," etc., the Greek terms used in the Gospels may have been influenced by early Christian references to Jesus' family phrased in Aramaic or Hebrew. Unlike Greek, these

Semitic languages in Jesus' time did not have precise vocabulary for a wide range of family relationships. Rather they reflected a tribal background, where members of the same tribe, clan, or family were considered brothers and sisters, no matter what their precise relationship. A classic example is the use of "brothers" in Gen 13:8 to describe the relationship between Lot and Abraham, when Lot was more precisely the nephew of Abraham. Drawing on this fact, one may argue that the men and women who are called the "brothers and sisters" of Jesus are being designated according to a loose Semitic "tribal" terminology and were, in fact, more distant relatives —therefore not children of Mary. I reiterate that one would not go this route unless one had other evidence that blood brothers and sisters were not involved.

Q. 68. Were not Catholics always taught that the brothers of Jesus were his cousins?

Catholics were taught that, but not "always." In the Western Church, St. Jerome became the spokesman for a solution that differed from the one offered in *The Protevangelium of James.* Jerome was interested not only in Mary's virginity, but also in Joseph's virginity as a symbol for encouraging the monastic, celibate life. Accordingly, he disliked the explanation offered by *The Protevangelium* that Joseph had children by a previous marriage. An alternative explanation was that they were the children of Joseph's brother or of Mary's sister. I shall not attempt to confuse you by the intricate arguments advanced for those theses. In any case, an approach that would make the "brothers and sisters" cousins of Jesus became the almost universal view in the Western Church, and that is why it is familiar to Roman Catholics. One should emphasize, however, that the Church *doctrine* concerning Mary's ongoing virginity never identified who the brothers were.

You may well be saying to yourselves, "How did the issue of whether Mary had other children become so important?" Some may even be asking more radically, "Who cares?" Yet this was already a divisive point in antiquity, for over against *The Protevangelium of James* there was a distinguished theologian, Tertullian, who identified the "brothers" as children born of Mary; but Jerome wrote with violent indignation against others who held that view.

As for the current importance of the question, the main advocacy for the view that Mary had other children begotten by Joseph came *after* the Protestant Reformation. It represented a developing attitude that the New Testament had to be read on its own terms (where "brothers and sisters" were mentioned) without the influence of subsequent tradition, whether that tradition be represented by *The Protevangelium* which spoke of Joseph's children by a previous marriage, or by a Church Father like Jerome who spoke of the cousins of Jesus. Yet behind the literalist approach to the New Testament there was another issue, namely, a struggle over the respective value of the married and celibate lifestyles. Many Protestants who maintained that Mary had children were implicitly criticizing the failure of Catholic priests to marry and have families. Many on the Catholic side who were arguing for the continued virginity of Mary were implicitly defending the value of celibacy as a gospel virtue, and therefore exalting the celibate priesthood and sisterhood. In comment on this last point, let me urge that we Christians who remain loyal to the tradition of Mary-Ever-Virgin must do so without denigrating marriage or family. We must be clear in our minds that, if after the birth of Jesus Mary had conceived in a normal way and borne other children, that would have been a saintly action blessed by God, even as was her decision to remain a virgin—a decision implied by the title "Ever Virgin."

As for the continuing dispute today, we may find some help in the answer given in the ecumenical book by Scripture scholars from various churches, *Mary in the New Testament* (ed. R. E. Brown, et al.; New York: Paulist, 1978), pp. 65–72. The authors of this book agree that the question of whether Mary had other children by Joseph is *not raised directly by the New Testament* nor answered without doubt therein. Rather, for intelligible reasons, depending on their *use of subsequent church insight,* Christians have emerged with different answers.

We Roman Catholics answer the question in the light of our church doctrine that Mary remained a virgin which, we hold, clarifies the uncertain picture presented by Scripture. We should abstain from considering unchristian those who interpret the New Testament differently; they should abstain from calling us nonbiblical when we speak of Mary-Ever-Virgin. The difference of belief is not directly over the Bible; the difference is in large part over the authority of tradition and church teaching.

Q. 69. Let me turn back from Mary to Jesus. Inevitably, much of what you commented on concerns Gospel *reports* about Jesus, their import, their accuracy, etc. But what can we know for certain about Jesus himself?

I take for granted that you are not talking about mathematical certitude or the certitude of the physical sciences, but the reasonable certitude or high plausibility that we have in human affairs—for example, the kind of certitude that I would have about the life and deeds of someone whom I know. Some scholars would give you the skeptical answer that we can know very little about Jesus. While I am optimistic about our knowledge of Jesus, I am not going to attempt to give you an exhaustive list or a complete rundown of his career, e.g., born in Bethlehem, raised at Nazareth, baptized by John, eventually beginning a ministry of preaching in parables and of healing, etc. I suspect you would want more detail than is possible in a simple question-response format, so I recommend as very helpful the article on "Jesus" in the *New Jerome Biblical Commentary* (Englewood Cliffs, NJ: Prentice Hall, 1990, pp. 1316–1328) by J. P. Meier. He is an excellent scholar and gives a well-balanced discussion with a detailed report of the Jesus of history. If you have some specific points, I would be glad to answer them to the best of my ability.

Q. 70. I do have a specific point. I want to know what Jesus thought of himself. Did he know he was God?

This is one of the rare occasions when I try to force people to rephrase their question, because the way it has been asked makes an intelligible answer almost impossible. I dislike intensely playing with words, and I have the same feeling of distrust that many others have when somebody says, "What do you mean by that word?" Yet

I must raise the issue here as to what the questioner means by "God." The question concerns Jesus, a Galilean Jew of the first third of the first century, for whom "God" would have a meaning specified by his background and the theological language of the time. By way of simplification (and perhaps oversimplification) let me say that I think that by a Jew of that period "God" would have been thought of as One dwelling in the heavens—among many other attributes. Therefore, a question posed to Jesus on earth, "Do you think you are God?" would mean did he think he was the One dwelling in heaven. And you can see that would have been an inappropriate question, since Jesus was visibly on earth. As a matter of fact the question was never asked of him; at most, he was asked about his relationship to God. One can get the flavor of the language and the problem in the scene in Mark 10:17–18: A man addresses Jesus as "good teacher," and Jesus answers him, "Why do you call me good? No one is good but God alone." You can see that there is a distancing between Jesus and the term "God."

Yet, quite rightly, you could point out that in another Gospel Thomas is lauded for addressing Jesus as "my Lord and my God" (John 20:28). The key to such phraseology is that it is found in the Fourth Gospel, written in the last years of the first century. I would say that by that time, under the impact of their quest to understand Jesus, Christians had in a certain sense expanded the meaning of the word "God." It no longer for them covered simply the Father in heaven; it covered the Son on earth. They had come to realize that Jesus was so intimately related to God, so filled with God's presence, that the term God was as applicable to him as it was to the Father in heaven. May I emphasize that this does not involve a change in Jesus; it involves a change and growth in the Christian perception of who he was. That growth continued so that at the Council of Nicea in the early fourth century Christians described the Son of God as "true God of true God." The impact of Jesus and the reflection that he caused changed all theological language for those who believed in him, including the term "God."

Now that I have clarified (I hope) the difficulty of the language, if you will permit me to rephrase your question in a way that I trust is true to your intent, perhaps I can try to answer it. Granted that the term "God" developed so that for Christians it represented a true insight into the identity of Jesus, your question, I think, could be phrased in this way: Did Jesus know that he had an identity which his followers later came to understand in terms of his being God? If he was God (and most Christians do agree on that), did *he* know who he was? I think the simplest answer to that is yes. Obviously there is no way of proving an affirmative answer because we do not have material describing all his life. Yet in the Gospel material given to us Jesus is always shown as being aware of a particular relationship with God that enables him to speak with awesome authority. There is never a scene in the Gospel portrait where he discovers something about himself that he did not know before. I realize that what I am saying runs against some popular views that would have Jesus discovering his identity at the baptism or some other time; but there is no evidence for such views. The baptismal scene is designed to tell the readers who Jesus is, not to tell him who he is.

Q. 71. But did he not grow in knowledge? Would he be human if he knew who he was during his whole life?

Let me start with the second part of that question. You and I are human beings. At what moment in our existences do we come to know that we are human and what that means? In a certain sense, do we not know that we are human from the first moment that we can think? At that moment we may not know all the ramifications of being human, and we certainly do not have the vocabulary to express what it means to be human. In fact, finding a definition of what it means to be human is a very difficult process. Yet we know that we are human.

By analogy, may one apply something similar to Jesus whom we believe to have been truly divine and truly human? Why would Christians not think that he knew who he was from the first moment his human mind functioned? That would not mean that he could give expression in human terms to what it meant to be divine —and that is why in the previous question I was so careful about terminology. We can know we are human without being able to find language to express it; Jesus could know he was divine without being able to find the human language that could express who he was. I think, by the way, that explains why the christology of the first three Gospels is largely implicit, i.e., not a christology where terms tell us who Jesus is but a christology where we find out who he is by hearing what he said and with what tonality he said it, and by observing what he does, and with what power and authority he does it.

Let me come back, however, to the first part of your question about his being human and therefore gradually increasing in knowledge. If Jesus seems to have known who he was throughout his whole recorded life, why would knowing his divine identity have prevented growth in his comprehension of how that identity interacted with a human life where growth, experience, the events of the ministry, and indeed his death, brought increased understanding of the human situation? One can suspect the existence of growth from a struggle such as that implied in the Gethsemane scene in Mark, where a Jesus who has challenged his disciples previously (10:38) to drink the cup that he was going to drink, now, in face of death, asks his Father if it is not possible that this cup pass from him. One could argue that that involves an internal struggle as the Son of God wrestles with the human experience of suffering and death. But we are guessing at that, and we are working from the analogy of our own human experience. No one knows the mysterious depths of the incarnation and its effects on Jesus internally. The Gospels were written to tell us what *we* should know of Jesus, not what he knew of himself.

Q. 72. I don't understand: You say you believe that Jesus was God; God knows all things; how can there be any question about what Jesus knew or about growth in knowledge?

I will have to answer that for you in almost philosophical language. According to scholastic philosophy, and the philosophy of Thomas Aquinas in particular, God's knowledge is not like our knowledge. Our normal form of knowledge is through concepts and judgments; in other words, we think. In scholastic philosophy, God's knowledge is immediate: He does not have ideas; He knows things intimately; He does not need to think in terms of putting concepts together and making judgments—it is a different form of knowledge. Therefore, the divine knowledge that Jesus would have possessed as the Second Person of the Trinity (if I may use a language that was not developed for several Christian centuries) really would not function in a human mind. In a famous passage in the *Summa Theologiae* (3,q.9,a.1,ad1) Thomas Aquinas observed: "If there had not been in the soul of Christ some other knowledge beside his divine knowledge, it would not have known anything. Divine knowledge cannot be an act of the human soul of Christ; it belongs to another nature." Therefore, you see it is not so easy to claim "God knows everything; therefore Jesus knew everything."

That same scholastic philosophy recognizes that occasionally there is in the human being immediate knowledge, something like the way God knows; and a primary example of immediate knowledge—not through concepts and abstractions—is our knowledge of ourselves. We know who we are by being what we are and not simply by thinking about what we are. It is exactly on that principle that in answering the question "Did Jesus know who he was," I saw no difficulty in saying he did. Karl Rahner phrased it in terms of the hypostatic union, i.e., the union between the Divine Person and the human nature. Without attaching myself to the theology of any one author and without getting involved in the more abstract expressions of systematic theology, I think it is fair to say: By being who he was, Jesus knew who he was.

Q. 73. Does that mean you claim Jesus had no more knowledge than we have?

No. As I insisted, his immediate knowledge of his identity, his knowing who he was, meant that he had the profoundest and most intimate knowledge of God's will. He was totally obedient to God's will and thus always in harmony with God's will; the New Testament describes him as without sin. Therefore he could speak with divine authority about what God wanted from us; we see this illustrated in the "Amen" sayings, where that word, instead of being used as a response acknowledging the truth of a statement, is prefaced to Jesus' statement demanding our acknowledgment. The New Testament description of people amazed at Jesus' speaking with authority and not like other teachers is again a recognition of a unique knowledge of God's will. The knowledge that flowed from Jesus' self-awareness of his identity with God during a human life is what caused Christians to believe that through him came the ultimate revelation of God. "In many and various ways in times past God spoke to our ancestors through the prophets; in these last days He spoke to us through a Son" (Heb 1:1–2).

Q. 74. But what about factual knowledge? Did not Jesus know things that were beyond ordinary human knowledge?

As I remember, the Spanish scholastic theologians associated with the University of Salamanca claimed an extraordinary range of knowledge for Jesus: he was the perfect soldier, scientist, artist, poet, etc. I see no evidence of this in the New Testament. People are astounded at his teaching with authority, not at a range of factual control. He would have spoken Aramaic and, presumably, Hebrew; he may have known some words and expressions in Greek because of the trade routes that passed through Capernaum; perhaps the Jews of Palestine also picked up a few Latin terms especially pertinent to Roman government and military exercises. But I see no reason to think he knew any languages beyond those that he learned, and he would have learned them with the parental accent. Whatever manual skills he possessed, I presume again that he would have learned from his parents. While we should not press too precisely the import of the statement, Luke who presents Jesus as divinely conceived has no problem in using of him the biblical description of growing in wisdom (Luke 2:40, 52).

Q. 75. Suppose we concentrate on knowledge of things pertinent to his mission; for instance, did Jesus know he was going to die?

In a way I always find that a curious question. So far as I can see, somewhere about or after age five, every member of the human race realizes that he or she is going to die, so that knowing that one is going to die is not an unusual form of knowledge. But I suppose the question really means did Jesus know the exact way and time he was going to die. Did he know he was going to be crucified?

There are in the Synoptic Gospels three famous predictions by Jesus of the death of the Son of Man (Mark 8:31; 9:31; 10:33–34). But two factors must be considered in evaluating those statements. First, they are written down in the Gospels thirty to fifty years after the events that took place on Golgotha or Calvary, and so it is very difficult to know in the process of Gospel development the extent to which those statements have been colored by Christian knowledge of what actually happened. Second, as Jesus encountered increasing hostility on the part of the religious authorities, he would surely have been sensitive to the possibility of a violent death. He had the example of prophets who had been persecuted and even put to death by the religious and political authorities. Living in Palestine and knowing the customs and laws of the Roman prefecture that ruled the land, he could have suspected or anticipated that a violent death would mean crucifixion, a standard Roman punishment. Therefore, some knowledge of the way in which he was going to die was not necessarily supernatural.

Q. 76. Let me ask, however, about knowledge that would clearly require supernatural help. Did Jesus know the future in detail? Did he have knowledge that he would rise from the dead?

I shall try to answer that question more comprehensively; but again let me point out the difference between a conviction that God would make him victorious (that is not only attested in the New Testament but totally harmonious with the faith and trust of Old Testament psalmists in moments of dire affliction) and a precise knowledge of how this would happen. It is the latter that you are interested in. Once again there are statements that Jesus made during the ministry that predict the resurrection of the Son of Man.

Here one would have to recognize a disagreement among Christian theologians. As I pointed out in my book *Jesus, God and Man* (New York: Macmillan, 1975; original 1967) where I wrestled head on with the question of how much did Jesus know, there were

Church Fathers in the early centuries who did not hesitate to admit ignorance in Jesus as part of the human condition. (Notice "ignorance," meaning a lack of knowledge—we should always avoid the pejorative term "ignorant" in reference to Jesus.) This was in harmony with the statement in the Epistle to the Hebrews (4:15) that he was tempted like us in everything, yet is without sin—that passage gives no indication that he was not like us in lack of knowledge.

However, there was another strain of Christian thought that insisted on all perfections for Jesus with the assumption that a lack of knowledge is an imperfection. One can argue about that: people who know everything are rarely admired, for it is the human condition, not a lack of due perfection, to have limited knowledge. In any case, in medieval scholasticism, especially in the writings of St. Thomas Aquinas, one finds the thesis that Jesus was given special forms of knowledge. Part of the reason for positing them is the recognition of Thomas (Q. 72 above) concerning the nontransferability of divine knowledge to a human mind which thinks in concepts. Therefore, knowledge useful for the human mind was supposed to have been given to Jesus. (Even then Thomas did not suppose that the human Jesus knew everything.) Thomas spoke of infused knowledge and of knowledge that was made available to the soul of Jesus through possession of the beatific vision all through Jesus' life. Many modern theologians have called into question such supernatural aids. In particular, Karl Rahner, Joseph Ratzinger, and Jean Galot (who would represent a wide spectrum of different theological approaches) have indicated that in their opinion it is not necessary to posit that Jesus had the beatific vision as that has been traditionally understood. In various ways they may posit an immediate experience of God (Q. 72), but would not insist on the communication of knowledge that Thomas posited through the beatific vision.

Those various theological speculations go beyond the New Testament evidence, but the theologians who allow ignorance or do not posit special additions of divine knowledge would be harmonious with the overwhelming view of biblical exegetes that Jesus shared many of the religious presuppositions of his time—presuppositions reflecting detectable limitations of knowledge with which the modern reader would not have to concur. For instance, Jesus seems to take literally that Jonah was three days and three nights in the belly of a fish (Matt 12:40), while we would understand the Book of Jonah as parabolic. In Mark 12:36–37 Jesus states that David spoke the opening line of Psalm 110, "The Lord said to my lord," with the assumption that David was thinking of the future Messiah. Few modern scholars would interpret the original meaning of the psalm in that fashion. In *Jesus, God and Man,* I cite other examples where Jesus seemingly shares the limited views of his era in regard to issues that are broadly religious. Thus one may argue that both biblically and theologically the position of limited knowledge seems defensible. It is worth emphasizing that to deny the full humanity of Jesus is just as serious as to deny the full divinity, and one may argue that it is truly human to be limited and time-conditioned in our knowledge. Thus we may have in Jesus the strange combination of absolute surety about what God wants of us if God's kingdom is to come, and a limited human way of phrasing the message.

Q. 77. Yet, if we admit limited human knowledge on Jesus' part, what about his preparations for the future? Some of those touch on the existence of the church.

That is a perceptive point and one of the reasons why I have always argued that a properly balanced appreciation both of the revelatory character of Jesus' ministry and of his limited human knowledge is so important for the Christian picture. If one posits revelation without limitations in human knowledge, one imagines a Jesus who foresaw all that would happen, including the full outline of the church, how it would develop, where it would be proclaimed, and various details of its liturgy and life. In short, one pictures a Jesus who gave us a blueprint for the church, and that is often quite close to the way the foundation of the church was understood in times past.

To such theorizing a New Testament scholar must raise the challenge: Where in the recorded words of Jesus in the Gospels is such a blueprint spelled out or even implied? In the four Gospels the word for "church" appears on Jesus' lips only twice. Since the word in Matt 18:17 clearly refers to the local community, one may say that only once in all the Gospels did Jesus ever speak about church in the larger sense, namely in Matt 16:18, "Upon this rock I will build my church," a statement that many think had postresurrectional origins. Thus there really is no Gospel evidence about detailed planning for or of the church, and the burden of proof has to lie on those who assume that Jesus had thought about all that.

Q. 78. Are you Bible scholars saying then that Jesus did not found the church?

Emphatically *I* am not making that negative statement. In my book *Biblical Exegesis and Church Doctrine* (New York: Paulist, 1985) p. 60, arguing strongly for the scriptural defensibility of the position that Christ did found the church, I referred to a debate between Karl Rahner and Hans Küng in which Rahner defended the position of Christ founding the church, which Küng regarded as inaccurate. Küng may know the biblical material more critically than Rahner, but I think Rahner's instinct was right. The foundation of the church by Christ is a fundamental part of Christian self-understanding. But founding the church need not mean that Jesus had detailed knowledge of what the church would be like or that he could have drawn up a blueprint for it. As an essential part of his ministry, Jesus called together followers and involved them in his work; and the risen Jesus poured out the Spirit on them so that they might continue the work. They constitute the continuity between Jesus and the church that emerged from their preaching. The church is no mere human institution, nor was its origin simply the result of a perceptive idea on the part of Jesus' followers. They understood that their calling believers together into a community was the direct continuation of what Jesus had done when he called them together and sent them out to continue his work. For that reason I insist on retaining the notion that Christ founded the church.

Q. 79. What about sacraments? Does not our understanding of the sacraments imply direct institution by Christ?

I think that question uses precisely the right term: "by Christ." The previous question spoke about the founding of the church by

Jesus, and I did not object because I think there is continuity between what Jesus did in his lifetime and the resulting church. Nevertheless the classical formulations for relating church realities to Jesus of Nazareth would have them stemming from *Christ.* The church teachers responsible for such formulations were not thinking simply of the Jesus of the ministry, i.e., exactly what Jesus said and knew before his crucifixion. They were thinking of the whole New Testament presentation of Jesus as the Christ, the Messiah, with postresurrectional insight. In answer to Q. 40 above I pointed out to what extent in the preaching phase before the Gospels were written down resurrection faith threw light on what had not been understood previously. Therefore, in discussing the institution of the sacraments the norm is not simply what Jesus said in the 20s in Palestine but the evidence for those sacraments in the whole New Testament.

Institution by Christ means that those actions we call sacraments are specifications and applications of a power that during his ministry and after his resurrection Jesus Christ gave to his church in and through the apostles—a power containing what was necessary to make God's rule or kingdom triumph over evil by sanctifying the lives of people from birth to death. The sacraments, we are saying, are no inventions of the church but are part of Christ's plan. I find no conflict between a modern biblical approach and "institution by Christ" so understood.

Q. 80. Be more specific: Did Jesus institute the sacrament of the eucharist at the Last Supper?

It has been standard Christian teaching that the eucharist was instituted by Christ (notice I come back to "Christ" as the classical terminology) at the Last Supper; and for Roman Catholics that was affirmed by the Council of Trent. Yet, once more, one does not have to hold that sitting at the Last Supper Jesus foresaw all that would develop from his statements about the bread and wine that he declared to be his body and blood. One does not have to think that he foresaw liturgical developments, the full practice of the eucharist in Christianity, or that he could speak about transsubstantiation.

It is interesting to note that, while in two of four accounts of the eucharistic words at the Last Supper "Do this in commemoration of me" is said (Luke 22:19; I Cor 11:24, 25), those words are absent from Mark and Matthew. So revered and cautious a scholar as the Dominican P. Benoit raised the issue of whether or not they could be a liturgical directive that appeared in the liturgy known to Luke and Paul, vocalizing an understanding that this eucharist was in fidelity to Jesus' mind. In such an interpretation "Do this in commemoration of me" would be part of the development of the Gospel message pertaining to Stage Two discussed in Q. 40 above.

Even without an appeal to that theory I would see a similarity between the institution of the sacraments and the founding of the church. Descriptions of both of these as actions of Christ are perfectly valid, but they do not have to include detailed foreknowledge by Jesus of all that would result. The Holy Spirit guided the developments and showed what was faithful to the mind of Jesus.

Q. 81. Does not one have an even more specific directive from Jesus about baptism—a directive that would show his foreknowledge of what would happen?

I presume you are talking about the last words in Matthew (28:19) where the risen Lord says: "Going therefore make disciples of all nations, baptizing them in the name of the Father and of the Son and of the Holy Spirit." But that very text illustrates the need for nuance. If that statement were made immediately after the resurrection in precisely those words, the Book of Acts would become almost unintelligible, for then there would be no reason why Jesus' followers should have had any doubt that he wanted disciples made among the Gentiles. Nevertheless, the debate over the acceptance of the Gentiles went on for the first twenty years of Christianity. Similarly if, as suggested by the Matthean text, such a developed baptismal form as "in the name of the Father and of the Son and of the Holy Spirit" was known from the immediate days after the resurrection, the common expression that we find elsewhere in the New Testament of baptizing in the name of Jesus becomes very hard to understand. Rather, what we find in Matthew as the last words on the lips of the risen Lord is an understanding of the Lord's mission to his disciples that came to clarity only after many years of struggling over the conversion of the Gentiles and after reflection showed the extent of the communality of the Father and the Son and the Holy Spirit, so that baptism in the name of Jesus had to involve the work of the Father and the Spirit as well.

Let me add an observation here that I will not develop at length. This statement is attributed to the *risen* Jesus, and statements attributed to him in the various Gospels differ more widely than statements of Jesus during the ministry. In answer to Q. 53 above I pointed out that while certainly the risen Jesus appears in a bodily way, there has been a tremendous transformation; and so we do not really know the extent to which the risen Jesus spoke words, i.e., audible, intelligible sounds, as means of communication. The differences in the statements attributed to him may mean that he revealed his will but that this revelation got its vocalization from those who received the revelation. That is speculation, however, and I do not wish to emphasize it.

Q. 82. Well, without explicit directives from Jesus, how did Christians come to baptize? What moved them in this direction?

To be frank, we do not know fully. In the first three Gospels, Jesus is never said to baptize anyone; in John 3:22 it is said that he baptized but that is denied in John 4:2. Nevertheless, *he* was baptized by John the Baptist; and that example may have led his followers, some of whom were disciples of John the Baptist, to recognize that just as Jesus showed his acceptance of John's proclamation by being baptized, so believers in Jesus show their acceptance of Jesus' proclamation by being baptized. And, of course, there is a saying associated with John the Baptist that while he baptized with water, there would come one who would baptize with the Holy Spirit (and with fire). Thus a baptism associated with a gift of the Holy Spirit may have been well planted in the expectation of Jesus' followers. Yet, although we do not know all the factors that caused them to understand baptism as faithful to the mind of Jesus, there are practices and sayings that make such a practice intelligible. The intelligibility would be greatly increased *if* there was already in practice a Jewish ritual washing of converts. The profession of belief in Jesus could have been understood as a type of conversion requiring such an initiation of all. But, once again, this is speculation and I put no emphasis on it.

What is interesting is the speed with which baptism must have become a universal practice among those who professed belief in Jesus. There is only one instance in the New Testament of believers in the postresurrectional period who have not been baptized, namely in Acts 18:24–19:7, where at Ephesus Apollos and some other disciples have had only the baptism of John. Were they possibly people who had come to believe in Jesus during his ministry but had not encountered postresurrectional Christian communities? (In the case of Apollos, he might have been converted to Jesus by such people.) Otherwise, in all our sources baptism seems to be the expected and accepted practice.

Q. 83. What did baptism mean for the early Christians?

Our standard Christian theology of baptism is really a conglomerate made up of different aspects of baptism that are mentioned in the New Testament. And so I would have to answer you that from the evidence baptism meant, at least by way of emphasis, different things for different Christians. In a relatively late New Testament work like the Gospel of John, a reference to being begotten by God, or born from above, is connected with water and Spirit. That implies that baptism was seen as the moment of the birth of the Christian, a birth not from a human mother, but from God Himself, a begetting that gives the believer God's own life. For Paul there is an emphasis on being baptized into the death of the Lord. And so baptism becomes our means of participating in the salvific death of Christ, and coming forth from the water of baptism can be compared in some ways to Jesus' coming forth from death. In language associated with baptism, I Peter speaks of the Gentiles now becoming the chosen people, so that in some ways baptism becomes an admission to the people of God.

If one asks about the earliest Christians, Acts 2 describes the baptismal demand put on Christians in relation to Peter's Pentecost sermon. Always with these scenes in Acts, we must recognize that the account is being written some sixty years after the event and being interpreted in the light of later theology. Yet it is interesting that the demand that is described as being placed on those who listen favorably to the apostolic preaching in Acts 2 involves *metanoia* (change of mind and heart and life associated with Jesus' proclamation of the kingdom) and an insistence on baptism (2:38). In other words, the preachers repeat something demanded by Jesus and then impose a second demand that he is never recorded to have made of followers during his public ministry. That additional demand for baptism has an interesting effect: The following of Jesus now comes to include a visible step. During Jesus' lifetime people were able to listen to him, be impressed by him, but go away without any visible sign that they had come to believe his proclamation of the kingdom. The demand for the visible sign by the preachers, a demand that has some historical content because otherwise baptism would not have become so widespread, is in a sense the first step toward organizing the believers into a visible community. The following of Jesus in his lifetime was informal; the instinct of the early Christians was to get a formal commitment that would identify the believer and would associate the believer with other believers. In other words, perhaps one of the first features of baptism was as the formative step in constituting a community. I do not pretend that I have covered all the New Testament aspects of baptism—only a few.

Q. 84. What about the eucharist? How did Christians come to celebrate eucharistic meals and what did those meals signify for them?

Once again there are different aspects of the eucharist emphasized in different New Testament writings. In response to Q. 80 above, I mentioned the traditional Christian teaching about the institution of the eucharist at the Last Supper, i.e., the sense that the eucharist is intrinsically related to the significance given by Jesus to the bread and wine at that supper as his body and blood. And certainly that must have been an early Christian understanding, for in I Cor 11:23–26 Paul mentions the eucharist (his only mention of it) precisely in relation to the night on which Jesus was given over or betrayed, and refers to the action the Gospels associate with the Last Supper. In Paul's understanding, each time the eucharist was celebrated, Christians recalled the death of the Lord until he comes. Notice it is not only a recalling or a re-presenting of the death of the Lord (something past in which we are given a share, even as for Paul there is baptism "into the death of the Lord") but an anticipation of something future. The future aspect of the coming of the Lord may have been a very early emphasis in the eucharist. When Jesus came back Christians would participate in the heavenly banquet. Indeed they may have conceived of Christ as finally returning in the eucharist. In the Dead Sea Scrolls community, a place was left vacant at the symbolic banquet for the Messiah in case God should raise him up during the meal. I call to your attention that the future aspect of the eucharist has been reintroduced into the Roman Catholic Mass as part of the proclamation of the mystery of faith after the consecration, for three of the four responses mention the future coming of the Lord.

Q. 85. What about John's Gospel? There is no eucharist mentioned at the Last Supper.

Right you are! And that is astounding in one way, since John's account of the Last Supper is the longest. In light of the fact that Paul regards it as a known tradition that Jesus performed the eucharistic action on the night before he died, John's omission may represent a deliberate choice to relate the eucharist to another part of Jesus' career—not necessarily denying the relationship to the Last Supper but seeing potentialities in earlier action.

When one thinks of the eucharist solely in terms of the Last Supper, it becomes something that Jesus does just before he dies, at the end of his life. Thus it stands in contrast to his ordinary ministry of preaching and of miraculous signs done to help and heal people. But John moves in the opposite direction by attaching the eucharistic words not to an unusual and solitary action at the end of Jesus' life but to the multiplication of the loaves, a sign done during Jesus' ministry. Jesus fed the crowds with bread; he nourished them. If the crowds had understood, that nourishment, although physical, did not have a primarily physical implication. The bread was the sign of a spiritual food that nourished the divine life given in baptism. In chapter 6 of John, after emphasizing the nourishing value of his revelation which is bread from heaven, Jesus stresses the nourishing value of his flesh and blood, which is John's eucharistic language. It is to John, then, that we owe primarily the emphasis on the eucharist as food: the food of eternal life.

While I am on the subject of eucharistic connections beyond the Last Supper, there is probably a relationship in some texts of the New Testament between the eucharistic breaking of the bread and the *appearance* of the risen Jesus *at meals* where he broke bread. Certainly that seems to be the implication of Luke 24:35 where the two disciples who were on the road to Emmaus recognized Jesus in the breaking of the bread. Such a relationship may have been a channel through which the emphasis on the real presence of Jesus came to the fore. In Christian theology, after all, it is the risen Jesus who is present in the eucharist, even as it was the risen Jesus who was present when the disciples broke bread. I am not saying that those post-resurrection meals were eucharists; I am saying that in reflection on the presence of Jesus at such meals, Christians may have come to understand a very important aspect of eucharistic theology. Thus, three meals (the Last Supper, the multiplication of the loaves, and post-resurrection meals) would have all left their mark on Christian thought about the eucharist. It is difficult to say which of these strains was the earliest.

By the way, I hope you see that my answers in regard to baptism and the eucharist are related to the non-blueprint approach that I took toward the origins of the church. Immediately after the resurrection, Christians did not have a total view of all aspects of baptism or of the eucharist, no matter how soon they began to perform those actions. Only over a period of time through the work of the Holy Spirit were they led to see different riches in what they regarded as gifts of Christ.

Q. 86. What was the relationship of the early Christians to the Jews?

Well, of course, all the first Christians were Jews. The Jewishness of Jesus and of the first to believe in him helps to explain the lack of a blueprint for the church. New structures did not need to be established because Judaism had its structures: it had its priesthood, sacrifices, liturgy, feasts, and administration. Jesus did not have to think about such issues, so long as they were open to the reformation of spirit demanded by the proclamation of the kingdom.

The Book of Acts (3:1; 5:12) reports that Peter and John and other members of the Twelve, in short, prominent figures of the first days, went to the Temple at the hours of prayer. The picture is given that their belief in Jesus caused no conflict with such Temple worship. Mark 12:29 would have Jesus instructing the readers, as a primary part of accepting the kingdom, to recite the prayer "Hear O Israel, the Lord our God, the Lord is one," the *Shema* or most basic of Jewish prayers. A hymn like the *Benedictus* (Luke 1:68-79) is in the format and style of Jewish hymns of the New Testament period, except for the sense of accomplished divine intervention, which Christians believed to have occurred in Jesus. One could give many more examples of the Jewishness of the earliest Christians.

Q. 87. What caused the separation of Christians from Jews?

That is not an easy question to answer, in part because we hear only one side of the dispute. There is no contemporary Jewish literature that discusses reactions by Jews who did not believe in Jesus to those who did believe in Jesus. Even later Jewish references, plausibly attributed to the second and third century, give evidence pertinent to this issue only obscurely and by indirection. If we work with the Christian references, combining them with common sense, the best available answer is that the separation of Christians from Judaism took place in different areas at different times with different tonalities and for different reasons.

A factor that certainly entered into the separation was the number of Gentile Christians intermingled with Jewish Christians in a given area. Synagogues consisting largely of Jews who did not believe in Jesus would have been most uneasy if there appeared in their midst Gentiles who claimed to be part of Israel because they believed in Jesus. At other places and times, entire synagogues of Jews may have come to believe in Jesus, or those who became Christian may have formed their own synagogue. Synagogues that were not Christian might not have felt impelled or been able to take action about such Christian synagogues. That could mean that some Christian synagogues could have gone on thinking of themselves as not formally rejected by Judaism for a considerable period of time.

Also, the intensity of the proselytizing proclamation of the gospel may well have been a factor. Did the Jews who came to believe in Jesus continue aggressively to evangelize Jews who did not—that would produce a division in a synagogue and might well lead to ejection. Another factor would seem to have been the way in which Christian believers expressed their evaluation of Jesus, i.e., their christological language. In my interpretation of the Fourth Gospel, where Christians confessed Jesus as God (John 20:28), the synagogue authorities seem to have reacted early and strenuously against Christian believers. The Johannine Christians were aggressive in argumentation and were understood to be making a mere man equal to God (5:18; 10:33). While Judaism was not a strongly creedal religion, it could scarcely tolerate attendance in the synagogues by those who worshiped two Gods; and ditheism is the way in which the Johannine Christian proclamation of the Word as God was understood.

Certainly there were other factors as well, but those that I have described may have hastened in some areas a separation of Christians from Judaism, indeed ejection from synagogues (John 9:22, 34; 16:2), whereas in other areas a more pacific social situation may have seen Christian Jews still attending the synagogue without major conflict. From the 50s until perhaps as late as 125–150, the process of separation continued until finally, in their own understanding, Christians and Jews were seen to represent different religions.

Q. 88. Was there any persecution of Christians by Jews?

Again I would remind you that for all practical purposes we have only Christian literature on this point. It is not inconceivable that what one side saw as persecution the other side saw as pedagogical correction. Paul in Gal 1:13–14 states that he persecuted Christians and that would have been in the early 30s in the Jerusalem or Damascus area. The Gospels have a prediction that believers in Jesus would be hauled before synagogue authorities and beaten (Matt 10:17; 23:34; Luke 12:11), and that would have been thought of as persecution. John describes not only the expulsion of Christians from the synagogue, but also the killing of Christians by Jews, interpreted as a service to God (16:2–3). Does that mean physical execution by Jewish authorities? (In II Cor 11:24 Paul says that he received from the Jews 39 lashes, a synagogue punishment.) Or does it mean that Jewish authorities denounced Christians to Roman authorities who then would have performed the execution? In part the answer to this depends on the likelihood that if the synagogue authorities ejected Christians and identified those ejected as no longer Jews, Rome would have become interested in this expelled group to know whether they were atheists and dangerous people—thus those expelled, having been deprived of the umbrella of Jewish identity, would have been subject to Roman execution. In my own judgment, it is likely that, either directly or indirectly, the synagogue authorities persecuted Christians vigorously in some areas, but not in others.

Q. 89. How large a role did the Twelve Apostles play in the Early Church?

In order to answer that question, I have to distinguish between the Twelve and apostles. The formula you used "the Twelve Apostles" appears in certain later New Testament works, but constitutes a shorthand description of persons who had two different roles.

An early formula was "the Twelve". It consisted of a group of men chosen by Jesus in his lifetime to symbolize the renewal of Israel. The only statement ever made by Jesus about the symbolism of the Twelve is that they were to sit on (twelve) thrones judging the twelve tribes of Israel (Matt 19:28; Luke 22:30). At the beginnings of Israel in the biblical account there stood the twelve patriarchs from whom the twelve tribes were descended. At this crucial moment in the renewal of Israel, there are these twelve men whom Jesus is choosing to symbolize the twelve tribes of the renewed Israel. They are eschatological figures—once for all—as their role as judges on heavenly thrones shows. Paul knows they were in existence already as of the time of resurrection appearances because he mentions them in I Cor 15:5. As a group, they are mentioned as active in the earliest descriptions of the church in Jerusalem (Acts 6:2). Indeed, they seem to have been primarily associated with Jerusalem, and that is not surprising. If they were to be part of the judgment, Acts 1:11–12 (plus Zech 14:4–5) may imply that Jesus was expected to return to exercise judgment on the Mount of Olives in Jerusalem. In the Book of Acts, the only members of the Twelve who are shown as active outside of Jerusalem are Peter and John; and that is partially confirmed by Paul who mentions Peter (Cephas) as a figure who came to Antioch (Gal 2:11) and who was well known to the community in Corinth, perhaps as one who had visited the city (I Cor 1:12; 9:5).

Turning from "the Twelve" to "apostles," we find that there are various meanings for "apostles" in the New Testament and certainly they are a wider group than the Twelve. Notice I Cor 15:5 and 7 where "all the apostles" is a wider group than "the Twelve." For Paul, at least in most uses of the term, the marks of an apostle are that one has seen the risen Lord and has been sent out to proclaim him, testifying in various places to him both by word and by suffering. Paul clearly thinks of Peter, one of the Twelve, as an apostle by this criterion (Gal 2:7). Whether he thought of all the Twelve as apostles by this standard, we are uncertain, but later New Testament works began speaking of the Twelve as apostles. Still later tradition began attributing to the Twelve careers of wide-ranging apostolates in various parts of the world, but we may well suspect that is legendary.

Q. 90. I always had the image that the Twelve Apostles ran the whole church. If they did not, how was the Early Church organized? Who ran it?

As I indicated in part in my answer to a previous question, I see the role of the Twelve as having symbolic importance for a renewed

Israel; and I think of the Early Church as the embodiment of the renewed Israel. The Early Church did not think of itself as a separate entity from Israel. Therefore, the Twelve rendered an important service to the unity of the early Christian communities. Nevertheless, they are not portrayed as administrators of communities. Indeed, the language of refusing to wait on tables in Acts 6:2 is a way of expressing a refusal to be involved in local administration of a Christian group. Neither as a whole, nor as individuals, are the Twelve portrayed as "running" a local church.

As to how the administration of local Christian groups developed, we are only partially informed. No single New Testament work attempts to describe this; rather we must depend on occasional haphazard references. In Acts 6:5 we see seven leaders being entrusted with the administration of the Hellenist Christian community, i.e., seemingly a group of Christian Jews who had a more radical attitude toward the Temple than another group of Christian Jews who are called Hebrews. While that chapter does not specify who the administrators of the Hebrew Christian community were, we find reference in later passages (Acts 12:17; 15:4, 13; 21:18) to James, the brother of the Lord, and the elders having a leadership role in the Church of Jerusalem. In I Thess 5:12, Paul speaks of some being over others "in the Lord" in the early community at Thessalonica, approximately A.D. 50. In a slightly later letter, I Cor 12:28, Paul mentions the existence of a number of charisms or gifts of God that would have implications for the leadership of the community in Corinth; his list contains "apostles, prophets, teachers, workers of miracles, healers, helpers, administrators, speakers in various kinds of tongues." We are not certain what "administrators" would do in such a community where there were also prophets and teachers; obviously, Paul the Apostle has authority over all. In the introduction to Philippians (1:1) Paul signals the existence of bishops (overseers) and deacons at that church, but we know nothing about what these figures did.

The Pastoral Letters (I Timothy, Titus) show an attempt just after Paul's time to get presbyter-bishops appointed in each town, alongside deacons. These presbyter-bishops (all? or most?) taught, administered community goods, surveyed the doctrine of individual members and their moral behavior, etc. *Didache* 15:1 (an early

Christian work, probably dating just after 100) regards the appointment of bishops and deacons as a replacement for the charismatic
offices of prophets and teachers. By the time of Ignatius of Antioch
(*ca.* A.D. 110) in some areas of the church of Asia Minor and Greece
there was developing already the pattern of one bishop overseeing a
whole local church, with presbyters and deacons under him. That
became the standard church pattern by the end of the second
century. For more detail see my book *Priest and Bishop.*

**Q. 91. What about the doctrine that the bishops are the successors
of the apostles?**

You are quite right. That is Catholic doctrine. I see no reason
why the New Testament evidence should be interpreted as imperil-
ing that doctrine when it is understood with proper nuance, and
provided one is exact in speaking of "apostles" and "bishops." I
stressed (Q. 89 above) that there is a distinction between the role of
the Twelve and the role of apostles, even if some men wore "both
hats." The doctrine does not suggest that the bishops are the successors of the Twelve as such. Indeed, since there are only twelve
thrones to judge the twelve tribes of Israel, there cannot be more
than twelve who have that role. In the Early Church there never was
a suggestion of replacing any members of the Twelve when they
died. (The replacement of Judas is because he gave up his role
among the Twelve, and there had to be twelve to begin the renewal
of Israel, since there were twelve patriarchs for the old Israel.)

The apostles, on the other hand, had the role of going out and
proclaiming the gospel and of forming communities of believers.
Someone had to take over the pastoral care of the communities
brought into being by the apostolic mission. As I indicated, by the
last third of the century and perhaps even slightly earlier, we find
the name "bishops" for those who played a role of leadership in
some communities. In the earlier stage there were plural bishops or
overseers in an individual community; in the later stage there was
the custom of having only one bishop per community. Therefore,
one may very correctly say that bishops took over the pastoral care
of communities founded by the apostolic evangelization and thus
were the successors of the apostles.

Apostolic succession concerns the fact that the bishops eventually took over the pastoral tasks of the apostles; it does not involve *how* the early bishops were chosen or appointed. We know little about that, not even being certain that there was a formal action designating them. On the analogy of a Jewish practice, and on the basis of the description of the designation of Timothy by Paul in the Pastoral Letters (II Tim 1:6) some have thought of the laying on of hands. Yet Timothy was not being designated as a bishop in the sense of administrator of a local community. His task was to get presbyter-bishops (plural) into communities, and therefore, a semiapostolic task. The laying on of hands may therefore have been the designation of him as an apostolic delegate. I Tim 5:22 has Timothy laying hands on others, but it is not clear that they are church administrators. Other information is found in Acts 14:23 which states that Paul and Barnabas (seemingly in the 40s) appointed elders in every church in towns in Asia Minor. We do not know whether that description in Acts is historically true in the lifetime of Paul; but certainly it would not have been included in Acts if there were not already in the 80s a tradition of such apostolic appointment of bishops. That tradition is also vocalized in the Pastorals where, as I have just pointed out, Paul is said to have appointed apostolic delegates like Timothy and Titus, who in turn appointed bishops. The same tradition is supported in the late 90s by *I Clement* 42:4 which has the apostles chosen by Christ going from city to city appointing their first converts bishops and deacons. That does not mean of course that all the presbyter-bishops of the Early Church were appointed by apostles, but there is a good chance that some were.

On the other hand *ca.* 100 *Didache* 15:1 tells Christians to *appoint for themselves* bishops and deacons. Further we may suspect that there were still other ways in which bishops could have been appointed. For instance, since the presbyter-bishops were married men, they could have arranged that their children succeed them. It is an area about which we do not have sufficient information. Eventually, of course, the church developed a regularized pattern of selection and ordination of bishops, and from the third century on that was universally followed.

Q. 92. How does such a developing pattern of choosing bishops affect the contention that ordination was a sacrament instituted by Christ?

In answering a previous question (Q. 79), I pointed out that "instituted by Christ" did not mean necessarily that in his lifetime Jesus had carefully thought out the sacramental system, or had foreseen the exact specification into different sacraments of the sanctifying power he gave to the church in and through the apostles. What he did at the Last Supper was the root, not only of the sacrament of the eucharist, but also of the sacrament of ordination. The doctrine of the Roman Catholic Church and of other churches that have a "high" estimation of ordination involves tracing to Christ the sanctifying pastoral power exercised in the episcopate, presbyterate, and diaconate, but not all the aspects of the discipline that developed. For instance, there is nothing in the words of Jesus at the Last Supper that specifies who are to "ordain" others, or in what manner. Even the common imagery that Christ himself ordained the Twelve at the Last Supper, with all its simplification, does not insist that he got up and walked around the table laying hands on each of them. Those whom the church eventually recognized as his bishops, presbyters, and deacons shared in the shepherding task that Jesus himself exercised toward those who followed him, and that the apostles exercised toward the first believers. The ordained ministry was not simply established by the church itself acting on its own authority; rather the existence of such an ordained ministry is an essential part of the continuation of the ministry of Jesus Christ and helps to make the church what it is. These essentials are affirmed by the doctrine that describes ordination as a sacrament instituted by Christ—not the modalities of choice by whom and how. They are fixed by religious practice.

Q. 93. I notice that when you were speaking of the role of the presbyter-bishops you did not mention the eucharist. Why is that?

For the most part I was attempting to describe the role of the presbyter-bishops in the New Testament; and therein the presbyter-bishops are never said to celebrate the eucharist. The closest one might come to a liturgical action attributed to presbyters would be the indication in James 5:14–15 that the presbyters of the church should be called in to anoint and pray over the sick. By the early second century, as we can see in the letters of Ignatius of Antioch, in the tripartite structure of the single bishop, plural presbyters, and plural deacons that he advocates, the celebration of the eucharist is assigned to the bishop alone, as also is the celebration of baptism. When he goes away, he may delegate others. Before that, however, in New Testament times we are very poorly informed about who celebrated the eucharist.

Since at the Last Supper in two accounts (Luke and Paul) Jesus says to those present, who were or included the Twelve, "Do this in commemoration of me," the presumption has been that the Twelve were remembered as presiding at the eucharist. But they could scarcely have been present at all the eucharists of the first century, and we do not know whether a person was regularly assigned to do this task and, if so, who that person was. (I should emphasize this point because various modern writers sometimes assert with re-markable surety that the head of the household celebrated the eu-charist. That is a guess; we have not a single text in the New Testa-ment that indicates that.) In *Didache* 10:7 we find that, despite a suspicion of wandering prophets, the author insists that they cannot be stopped from "eucharistizing." If that means "to celebrate the eucharist" rather than simply "to give thanks," then in some places the prophets may have had a eucharistic role in the liturgy (see also Acts 13:1–2). Eventually, of course, the church regulated and regu-larized the celebration of the eucharist; and, indeed, that was a development that was inevitable if communities were to be pro-vided regularly with the bread of life. They could not depend on haphazard provision.

Q. 94. If the person who celebrated the eucharist was not desig-nated in a regular way in New Testament times, does not that mean

that we would be free today to have certain flexibility about who celebrates the eucharist?

Let me remind you that I stressed our ignorance of New Testament times. Our documents do not give us the information to state that the celebrant of the eucharist was determined according to a rigidly fixed pattern; but I did not affirm that no such pattern existed. We simply cannot document the situation.

But suppose you are right, and there was no pattern rigidly fixed in all the churches as to the celebrant of the eucharist. There still must have been some type of church recognition; the people who came to the eucharistic meal must have accepted in some way that an individual speak the words of the Lord. (Even on that point, while we have an indication that the words of the Lord were spoken because of their citation, not only in the Gospels, but in I Cor 11:23–26, we are not really sure of *how* the eucharist was celebrated in New Testament times.) To my mind that means that church recognition is essential for the role of the eucharistic celebrant; and that is why the church has insisted on ordination, which is its established way of giving public acknowledgment to who can and should celebrate the eucharist.

As I have stated, the church regularized the manner of ordination and that regularization is binding because it represents church acknowledgment. If your question asks whether the church could recognize another way of designating a eucharistic celebrant, my personal answer (and it has no more value than a personal opinion) is that the church could do that. But in "the church" I would most certainly include the official authorities of the church—in Roman Catholicism that would be the pope and the bishops. I think the church thus understood could establish another way of acknowledging eucharistic ministers besides a formal action of laying hands by a bishop, although I do not think the church is likely to do that. What I would judge intolerable is that someone appoint himself or herself as the celebrant of the eucharist or that some small group constitute their own members celebrants in disunity from the larger church. It was precisely to prevent such aberrations that a regularized practice developed. A recognition that the church situation was a developing one in New Testament times does not mean that all developed specifications are revocable or optional and can simply be dispensed with. The Holy Spirit continued to act in the church after the first century and the later specifications can be looked on as the work of the Holy Spirit guiding the church to what it should do. If the church wishes to change a practice, it would need the guidance of the Holy Spirit to do so; and that decision would have to be expressed in a public and universal way.

Q. 95. In all of this you have not mentioned the term priesthood. Why is that?

Again, I have been concentrating largely on the New Testament picture and the immediate post-New Testament picture. In all that literature, the term "priest" is never applied to a Christian minister. When people ask me what did Jesus think about priests, my standard answer is that when the texts relevant to Jesus' attitude refer to priests, they are talking about those who functioned in the Jewish Temple offering sacrifice. There is no indication whatsoever that Jesus used the term "priest" to refer to his followers or to a ministry of the future community. Once again, that does not mean that the ministry of the future community is not instituted by Christ. The ministry flows from the actions of Jesus; and since Christian ministerial priesthood is intimately associated with the eucharist, it flows from what he did at the Last Supper. But the *terminology* of priesthood would have reflected Jesus' own experience as a Jew, and there were Jewish priests already.

In the later New Testament period we find the whole Christian people who are "God's own possession" being called a "royal priesthood" (I Pet 2:9). That gave rise to what is erroneously called "the priesthood of the laity"; rather it is a priesthood of the whole people of God, not to be minimized by later distinctions between clergy and laity—a priesthood where the sacrifice offered is a goodness of life that glorifies God (I Pet 2:12 and 2:5). We find also Jesus himself being referred to as a priest, explicitly in the Epistle to the Hebrews. Yet even that epistle shows an awareness of the much more frequent use of the term for the Jewish levitical priesthood because it has to explain that Jesus is not a levitical priest but a priest according to the order of Melchisedek, the priest-king of Jerusalem who was not a Levite and whose priesthood did not depend on his genealogical origins. So far as I know, it was only *ca.* 200 that the term "priest" started to be applied to the bishop and only still later was it applied to the presbyter.

This observation explains why some Protestant churches who insist on using New Testament language alone refuse to call their ministers priests; they do not regard it as New Testament terminology. When in the post-New Testament period the language of priesthood did begin to be applied to the bishops and presbyters, it brought with it a certain Old Testament background of the sacrificing levitical priesthood. The introduction of that language was logically tied in to the development of language for the eucharist as sacrifice. (Notice once again that I speak of the development of language. I think there were sacrificial aspects in the early understanding of the eucharist; but I have no indication that the eucharist was called a sacrifice before the beginning of the second century.) When the eucharist began to be thought of as a sacrifice, the person assigned to preside at the eucharist (bishop and later presbyter) would soon be called a priest, since priests were involved with sacrifice.

Q. 96. Is "priest" then just an added term for "bishop" and "presbyter"?

No, I would not say that. A development of terminology of this sort reflects a development in understanding a reality and helps to bring out aspects of it. The descriptions of the presbyter-bishops in the Pastoral Letters in terms of shepherding and administrative care catch an important part of the Christian ministry. But the rooting of that ministry in Jesus Christ himself is not clear in the Pastorals. When the minister starts to be called a priest, then the relationship between the presbyterate and the priesthood of Jesus Christ exercised in his sacrificial death, according to the Epistle to the Hebrews, becomes clearer. The presbyter is more than a shepherd and an administrator; the presbyter participates in the great intercessory act of Jesus Christ, even as the eucharist makes present again the death of the Lord until he comes.

I have mentioned that some Protestant churches do not use the term priesthood for their ministry; and I suspect that practical differences of attitude that separate Catholics and Protestants in regard to ministry may reflect a different idealism corresponding to the terminology of ministry and priesthood. In their ministry the presbyter-bishops of the Pastorals are to be ideal models for the Christians of the community, not only in virtues, but in the ordinary way of life. They are chosen because they know how to run households, to be good husbands and good fathers. The involvement of such presbyter-bishops in ordinary life is taken for granted. On the contrary, the Old Testament levitical priest, when he offers sacrifice, is to be removed totally from the secular. He is to be specially washed, clothed in special vestments, and set apart from the community because he is entering into contact with God, the All Holy. I would judge it inevitable that when the term priesthood began to be employed for the Christian bishop and presbyter, some of this demand for separation from the secular and for a unique holiness removed from the ordinary patterns of life had to become part of the Christian ideal for the presbyter-bishop. In my book *Priest and Bishop* (New York, Paulist, 1970) I pointed out that this has created a tension in the expectations of Catholics about their priests. As ministers who have to be involved with the lives of those for whom they are to be shepherds, there is a demand for the clergy to share in ordinary life and problems; but as priests who are called to represent the community in a special way before the holiness of God, there is also a demand that they be somewhat separated and uniquely dedicated to God.

As I understand the position of Hans Küng, he regards the introduction of Old Testament levitical priestly ideas into the Christian ministry as an aberration and would dispense with it. I take the opposite view that in God's providence this was a way of preserving a unique value from Israel and that the tension, while difficult, is healthy. But then my whole approach to the church as preserving tensions is shaped by my understanding of the incarnation, which preserves the tension of the divine and the human in the one Jesus. I recognize that there are many in our times who prefer to dissolve the tensions of two expectations by getting rid of one. For me that is an impoverishment of Christianity. Throughout my responses you can detect that I have a sense according to which Christianity, stemming from the incarnation, has to preserve attitudes that are in tension—the incarnation, involving the fully divine and the fully human in Jesus, is a primary tension. The Scriptures, as entirely words written by human beings and yet stemming uniquely from God, involve a tension. The church and the sacraments, instituted by Christ and yet going beyond any blueprint or expressed detailed plan uttered by Jesus, involve a tension. So also does a ministry, identifiable with the community from whence the minister springs and yet set apart for service in the presence of God and representing Christ the priest.

Q. 97. You have not been specific about Peter's role in church leadership; would the early Christians have recognized him as the head of the church?

Before I answer that, let me urge you to be a bit cautious about the term "the head of the church." In New Testament language that term is used for Christ, particularly in the Colossians and the Ephesians material. The church is the body and Christ is the head. Even with the respect that we have for the pope as the successor of Peter according to the insights of Roman Catholic doctrine, we should always make clear that this leadership supplied by the pope does not supplant our agreement with the general Christian faith that Christ is the unique head of the church. Christ exercises that headship in part through papal leadership, so that the pope is no rival to Christ.

But coming back to the thrust of your question, let me comment on two levels: the first is on the level of what Peter does during his lifetime, and the second is on the level of symbolism in sayings about Peter. *On the level of his lifetime,* in all four Gospels Peter emerges as the most important disciple of Jesus in terms of being mentioned most frequently, and speaking most frequently. Indeed, very often, in all the Gospels he is the spokesman for the group of the Twelve and the immediate followers of Jesus. In our current approach to the Gospels we know that there is a basic content that comes from the time of Jesus and a development of that content in the course of Christian preaching. (See response to Q. 40 above.) Therefore, whether the portrait of Peter's activity in the ministry of Jesus is entirely historical in the sense that he did all these things so prominently during Jesus' lifetime, or is a simplification produced by Christian preaching, we are still being told about the importance of Peter during his lifetime, since much of the development of the Gospel tradition through preaching would have taken place during those years between the crucifixion of Jesus in the early 30s and the death of Peter in the mid-60s.

Peter's prominence by way of activity after the resurrection is portrayed in the Book of Acts; and if we take the modern approach to Acts as a work of the 80s, at least we learn that in the 80s Peter was remembered as the most active of the Twelve in Jerusalem and, indeed, outside Jerusalem in the first years of the Christian movement. This is confirmed indirectly by the Pauline letters. Paul preached to churches in Galatia, and when he writes Galatians, he simply assumes that they know who Cephas (Peter) is, mentioning his presence in times past at Jerusalem and at Antioch. Similarly, when he writes I Corinthians and he discusses the privileges of an apostle he mentions Cephas and his wife (I Cor 9:3). One may make an intelligent guess that everywhere among Christian communities in the period of the 60s Peter's name would have been known and he would have been looked on as a figure of importance. (The amount of importance given to Peter would have varied somewhat according to whether he had visited that area or not.) There is solid support for asserting that he would have been acknowledged as the most important of the Twelve and as having taken part in major Christian decisions pertinent to the extent of the mission of pro-claiming the gospel.

If I may move to *the level of symbolism,* probably already during his lifetime, but certainly in documents that circulated after his lifetime, Peter became the symbol of pastoral leadership in diverse regions. Let me emphasize that the Gospels of Matthew, Luke, and John were all most likely written after Peter's death and that therefore texts in them concerning Peter have an importance for revealing the mindset of the last third of the first century pertinent to this figure. In Matt 16:16–18, we have the famous passage in which Jesus says to him, "Blessed are you, Simon Bar-Jona! For flesh and blood have not revealed this to you, but my Father who is in heaven. And I say to you, you are Peter; and upon this rock I will build my church, and the gates of hell shall not prevail against it." In that statement, Peter is raised up as the recipient of divine revelation that enables him to proclaim Jesus the Christ, the Son of the living God. Because of that revelation and proclamation, he is portrayed as the rock on which the church will be built. That certainly implies a memory of Peter as a great preacher, as one who vocalized the correct understanding of the identity of Jesus, which constitutes the gospel, and as one who through his preaching and faith was the foundation of the church as Matthew knew it.

In Luke 22:31–34, as Jesus is at the Last Supper and faces the prospect of his death, he announces that Peter will deny him before the cock crows; but first Jesus utters a special prayer for Peter: "Simon, Simon, behold Satan asked to test you (plural) like wheat, but I have prayed for you (singular) that your faith might not fail. And you, when you have turned around, strengthen your brothers." In that portrayal, Christians of the last third of the first century would be taught that Jesus saw in Peter a special instrument for strengthening the faith of his other followers, and that in the crisis provoked by Jesus' crucifixion and resurrection special prayers for Peter would enable him to survive and play this instrumental role so significant for the beginning and endurance of the church.

In John 21:17–19, the risen Jesus is portrayed as speaking to Simon Peter, testing his love, and then assigning to him a role in feeding the sheep. This is an extraordinarily important passage in a Gospel that has already claimed a unique primacy for Jesus as the Good Shepherd. Almost by way of concession, Peter, through his love for Jesus, is granted shepherding in the flock that remains the property of Jesus. All three passages written for different communities confirm the ongoing symbolism of Peter as the embodiment of faith, proclamation, pastoral care, and continued support in the church.

Q. 98. But doesn't Paul resist Peter? Would Paul recognize Peter's supremacy?

Notice that when I was talking about Peter I did not say he was the *only* leader in the church. I was careful to state that in his lifetime all would have agreed that he was the most prominent of the Twelve, and that after his lifetime his image had enormous symbolic value for the foundation and overall pastoral care of the church. Yet in other areas of church activity Peter's role would have been limited. For instance, there is no solid New Testament evidence for Peter as the administrator of a local church, whether that be Jerusalem, Antioch, or Rome—the administrator later called a bishop. And other figures besides Peter had leadership roles in the church. For example, if we study the church situation in Jerusalem about 49—the period of the so-called Council of Jerusalem—we would have to recognize that there were people with different importances involved in that discussion concerning the issue of converting the Gentiles without insisting that they become Jews first (i.e., without insisting that Gentile men be circumcised). Peter had a unique importance as the most prominent of the Twelve; James had unique importance as a relative of Jesus who was the leader of the Jerusalem community; Paul had unique importance as a great evangelizer of the Gentiles whose apostolic ministry had crystallized the issue of Gentile conversion. Each of those figures had the right to express his mind, and they may not have agreed on their approaches to the issue. Fortunately, they all did agree on what we would call the bottom line, the possibility of admitting the Gentiles without circumcision.

Now you asked me did not Paul resist Peter? Yes, he did in two instances that we know of. In the case of the Jerusalem situation about which I have just been talking, Paul went to Jerusalem convinced that he had proclaimed the one true gospel of the grace of Jesus Christ for the conversion of all; and it is clear from his words that no matter what Peter, or James, or any other human being (or even any angel) would say, Paul was not going to change his gospel. Nevertheless, he had to deal with Peter and James and the Jerusalem authorities. He disparagingly referred to them as so-called pillars of the church (Gal 2:9), but even that disparaging reference has an implication about Peter's importance. Evidently, there were people who thought him to be a "pillar of the church"; and even if Paul did not share their admiration, he still had to go to Jerusalem and deal with Peter because of the importance of the Jerusalem authorities. They had the power of breaking *koinonia* or communion with Paul, and for Paul that would have undone his work in the sense of creating a division in the following of Christ. Fortunately, as I said, the *koinonia* was preserved at Jerusalem (Gal 2:9).

The other time that Paul had a struggle with Peter was subsequently at Antioch where another issue came into dispute (Gal 2:11–14). Were those Gentile converts who had been admitted without circumcision bound by any of the Jewish food laws? At least that seems to be a way of translating the dispute about Peter's eating with the uncircumcised and changing his mind under pressure of men from James. When Peter yielded to those who forbade table fellowship with Gentile Christians, Paul judged that Peter had betrayed the gospel. This was obviously a moment of ire and represented a major disagreement among two Christian leaders, or even among three. My overall analysis is that Paul insisted that the Gentiles were not bound by the food laws; men from James insisted that they were; and Peter held an intermediate position where the issue was a free one, but he would rather side with the men from James than divide the community.

I would regard this as clear proof that Paul would not have had to accept all Peter's views and Peter did not have to accept all Paul's views. And I think it urgent in Christianity today that we recognize there can be matters of legitimate dispute among Christian theologians and even among Christian leaders. What is extremely important in relation to the Peter-Paul situation, however, is that when it came to the essentials of the faith about Christ in I Cor 15—a passage where Paul spoke about the death and resurrection and appearances of Jesus—he mentioned first the appearance to Cephas (Peter), and then an appearance to James, and then an appearance to himself. In relation to all that, Paul said, "So do we preach and so do you believe." He recognized that in the essentials of the proclamation about Christ, he himself and Peter and James preached the same basic message, and Christians had to believe it. If a legitimate diversity must be recognized in Christianity today, so must the need for a uniformity in essentials. Thus the disagreements between Peter and Paul do not, in my judgment, detract from the importance of Peter in the specific ways I have mentioned.

Q. 99. You said that Peter is not called a bishop in the New Testament. I thought Peter was the first of the bishops of Rome.

By the end of the second century, we begin to get the lists of bishops of major cities. In the list of the bishops of Rome given by Irenaeus, for instance, Peter is listed first. Yet one must ask what that means. Somewhere in the second century (probably around the middle of that century) the Roman church developed the structure of a single bishop and plural presbyters, even as other churches had developed or were developing that structure during the second century. From that moment on, the presbyter acknowledged as the leader of the Roman church, especially in matters pertaining to relations to other churches, was called bishop. Before the development of the single bishop, various matters at Rome seem to have been dealt with by a group of presbyters; but inevitably in that group an individual stood out as a natural and implicitly recognized leader for a specific purpose.

For instance, putting together later information, we can recognize that a letter sent by the Church of Rome with admonitions to the Church of Corinth, around the end of the first century, was written by Clement, a presbyter of the Church of Rome. It is quite unlikely that Clement was called *the* bishop of Rome; he was closer in modern terminology to the executive secretary of the church. Nevertheless, since he was remembered as the most prominent of the presbyters of his time, his name appears in the list as a bishop of Rome.

Similarly, I would suggest that in the 60s, when Peter came to Rome, this first among the Twelve was the most prominent figure in the Roman Church. In the language of the end of the second century, that would have caused him to be listed as the bishop of the Church of Rome, even if Peter's contemporaries in the 60s might not have used that term for him. What I am saying is that those lists of bishops have preserved for us the most prominent authoritative figures in the history of a particular church, even before the terminology of only one bishop was used. Thus, I am in no way taking away from the importance of Peter, or from his stay in Rome, when I point out that it is anachronistic to think of him as a local bishop. Indeed, since the task of the bishop was to administer a small congregation and live among them, I would say that the importance of Peter ranged far above that: as first of the Twelve he represented the wholeness of the renewed Israel and the role of judging all the Christian people of God.

Q. 100. The most important question is: Would Christians of New Testament times have looked on Peter as the pope?

Again I must plead for the recognition that it takes a while for terminology to develop, that the terminology of the later church was not ready-made in the first century, and that when later terminology came into existence it had implications more specific than what may have been understood by first-century Christians. For instance, when the term "pope" began to be used in later centuries for the bishop of Rome, that term vocalized major developments in the history of the Roman bishop. Rome was the capital city of the Empire, and so the Church of Rome took on the mantle of the church of the most important city in the world. It was at Rome that the apostles Peter and Paul were martyred; and thus in a very real way the see of Rome became *the* apostolic see, possessing in its heritage the remains and legacy of the two most important apostles in Christian memory. In the second century in particular, the Roman presbyters had played a remarkable role in resisting heretical ideas and insisting on the purity of the Christian faith, so that the see of Rome had become a symbol of the tradition preserved in its purity. All these factors colored the description of the bishop of Rome as the pope, since they contributed to an understanding of the Holy See as having responsibility toward and for the scattered churches of the empire and for preserving orthodox faith.

Now, as a questioner in the twentieth century, when you ask was Peter considered to be the pope, you are asking with an even richer tradition behind the term "pope." In particular, in the mod-

ern background there lies the declaration of Vatican Council I that
the pope has jurisdiction over every Christian. Obviously, first-century Christians would not have thought in terms of jurisdiction or
of many other features that have been associated with the papacy
over the centuries. Nor would the Christians of Peter's lifetime have
so totally associated Peter *with Rome,* since it was probably only in
the last years of his life that he came to Rome. Nor would their
respect for the church at Rome have been colored by the martyr-
dom of Peter and Paul there, or by a later history of the Roman
church's preservation of the faith against heresy.

Perhaps the proper way of phrasing an answerable question
pertinent to the 60s is not, "Would the Christians of that period
have looked on Peter as the pope?", but "Would Christians of that
period have looked on Peter as having roles that would contribute
in an essential way to the development of the role of the papacy in
the subsequent church?" I think the answer is yes, as I tried to
explain in response to a previous question where I pointed out the
roles that Peter had in his lifetime, and the symbolisms attached to
him even after his death. To my mind, they contributed enormously to seeing the bishop of Rome, the bishop of the city where
Peter died, and where Paul witnessed to the truth of Christ, as the
successor of Peter in care for the church universal.

In the ecumenical book done by scholars of different Christian
churches, *Peter in the New Testament* (eds. R. E. Brown et al.; New
York: Paulist, 1973), we used the language of a Petrine trajectory. I
think that is a good term, for it conveys the image of a long line of
development starting out in Peter's lifetime and continuing into the
subsequent church. I see the papacy on a line of development from
Peter. Interestingly, the Gospel memory preserves some of the failures of Peter as well as statements indicating his authority. It has
not forgotten his chastisement by Jesus for not understanding
(Mark 8:31–33) and his denials of Jesus. That can be very helpful to
us Roman Catholics who believe firmly in the pope as the vicar of
Peter in carrying out Christ's care for the church. Even as Peter at
times failed, so there have been holders of the papal office who have
been significant failures, and even scandals. None of that detracts
from the essential symbolism attached to the Petrine office, a symbolism of a strengthening in faith, of a foundational rock that en-

ables the church to stand against the forces of evil, and of a shepherd or pastor who, having been tested by the demand for love of Christ, has been commissioned to care for the flock of Christ.

Q. 101. From what you have been telling us, the church in New Testament times would have been a lot different from the church today, wouldn't it?

In many ways that is right. Certainly the private homes where those early Christians met would have been a lot different from our church buildings, and the style of the meetings and what we could call liturgies would have been different even if there were hymns and prayers. As I mentioned, they had baptism and the eucharist. Yet, our theology of baptism and our theology of the eucharist would be a composite of ideas that might have been quite separate in New Testament times, in the sense that no one given community would have had all those ideas. The early Christians would have had different forms of church leadership, which were developing rapidly toward the end of the first century. Interestingly, some of the churches would already have been speaking of bishops, but those bishops would have been different in many ways from the bishops of the large dioceses that we know today. And I suppose there are many other features implying difference that could be mentioned. After all the church consists of human beings living in time; and, while it draws its identity from Christ, the church changes over the course of centuries according to the needs and patterns of life of the individuals that make it up. Hebrews 13:8 says that "Jesus Christ is the same yesterday, today, and forever." No New Testament book ever claims that the church is the same yesterday, today, and forever.

Curiously, however, having said that, I would insist that what strikes me is not so much the change but the continuity that exists between that first church and the church today. We believe it is the same Spirit that the risen Christ gave to his disciples that vitalizes the church today. The basic sacrament of baptism gives us God's life and makes us children of God even as it did for the first Christians. The same eucharistic body and blood feeds that life even as it did for the first Christians. The styles of administration and the names we give to those who exercise pastoral care may have varied, but the same authority for making God's kingdom and rule present in the world that Christ communicated to the church in the person of his apostles functions in the church today.

Perhaps I can make all this concrete in a way that I have found meaningful. The oldest preserved Christian document is Paul's first letter to the Thessalonians. It was written about the year 50. It is an extraordinarily fascinating exercise to ask ourselves this question: Suppose we twentieth-century Christians were to be taken back in time and walk into a meeting of the converts made by Paul in Thessalonica when that letter was being read to them for the first time. As we heard it, would we recognize that we were among Christians who had the same faith that we have? Would we know that we were not in a Jewish synagogue or a pagan meeting place but truly in a Christian church? It would not take us two minutes to decide, for in the first five verses of the oldest preserved document written by a Christian there is already mention of God the Father, the Lord Jesus Christ, and the Holy Spirit. Already there is mention of the work of faith, the labor of love, and endurance in hope. Your question involved the differences between the church of New Testament times and the church of today. An essential sameness is that we proclaim the same Father, the same Jesus Christ, and the same Holy Spirit; and that we still value above all else faith, hope, and love.

APPENDIX: EXPRESSING CATHOLIC FAITH SO THAT BIBLICAL FUNDAMENTALISTS WILL NOT MISUNDERSTAND IT

In Q. 31–33 in this volume I responded to questions about biblical fundamentalism, and those responses covered such items as the origins of fundamentalism, why Roman Catholics are now encountering it, and some suggestions for countering it. Recently as I have lectured, questions concerning fundamentalism have become much more frequent, indicating that the issue is becoming of greater concern. In particular, I am struck by the number of people, Catholics and mainline Protestants, who come up at the end of a question period where the issue of fundamentalism has been raised to tell me that a member of their immediate family has ceased to come to church with them and has gone over to a fundamentalist group.

Beyond what is mentioned in the responses, there is an aid that does not fit well into the question-and-answer format, and that in fact I have never used as a response but as part of a lecture given on fundamentalism. Roman Catholics often are often nonplussed when tenets of their faith are queried by biblical fundamentalists, sometimes polemically, but more often in conversation. Many Catholics have had items of their faith like the mass, sacraments, pope, Mary, and the saints explained in a phraseology from their catechisms, but nothing in that training equips them to handle the objection that such beliefs are nonbiblical. Their first reaction to a

137

fundamentalist probing may be to respond in terms of church teaching—a response that confirms the fundamentalist in the opinion that Catholic beliefs are totally foreign to the Bible. It might help if Catholics were able to speak about these issues in biblical language that fundamentalists might understand. In Q. 33 I warned against swapping proof texts, or attacking fundamentalists, or trying too suddenly or too simply to convert them; but this is a different issue. Catholics would feel more self-confident if they understood the Bible-relatedness of the doctrine being queried, and biblical fundamentalists might at least realize that their understanding of Catholic doctrines is too simplified if those doctrines were intelligibly phrased in a biblical atmosphere.

Consequently I have written below ten paragraphs dealing with doctrinal issues most often queried by fundamentalists, explaining how one might describe the Catholic understanding as related to biblical faith. At the beginning of each paragraph I have printed in boldface the issue of *their* biblical faith that fundamentalists are concerned to defend and within the same parenthesis, distinguished by *vs.,* the issue of Catholic faith that bothers fundamentalists as they understand it. I emphasize that my explanatory paragraphs are one person's attempt to phrase the Catholic faith on these points biblically; and although I have shared my wording with others to be sure I have not misrepresented Catholic doctrine, I am certain that improvements can be made. Indeed, I hope that my limited efforts might encourage others along the same line. As I have indicated above, in no way am I expressing the fullness of Catholic faith on the subjects discussed; I am treating only aspects of those subjects that are of most concern to biblical fundamentalists.

If readers find these paragraphs useful, they are circulated separately in convenient brochure format as an issue of *Catholic Update* (May 1990; CU–0590) by St. Anthony Messenger Press in Cincinnati.

1. (**The Sufficiency of the Bible** vs. a teaching church) The Roman Catholic Church considers itself a biblical church in the sense that it acknowledges and proclaims the Bible to be God's word. In the teachings of Moses and the prophets, and in the teachings of Jesus proclaimed by the apostles, *to which the Scriptures bear witness,* the Catholic Church confesses that God has revealed

Himself to humankind in a unique way. It acknowledges the sufficiency of that revelation witnessed by the Bible in the sense that no
new revealer or no new special revelations are necessary for men
and women to find the will of God and the grace of salvation. If
great attention has been given to the teaching of the ongoing church
in Roman Catholicism, that teaching is not presented in terms of a
new revelation but as the result of the church's continuing task to
proclaim the biblical revelation in light of new problems in new
generations. In carrying on that task, the church regards itself as the
instrument of the Paraclete-Spirit promised by Christ which would
take what he had given and guide Christians along the way of truth
in subsequent times (John 16:13).

2. (**The One Mediator Jesus Christ and Faith in Him** vs. good
works and prayers to saints) The Catholic Church proclaims to its
people that justification and redemption came through the grace
given by God because of the death and resurrection of Jesus.
Human beings cannot earn redemption or salvation; neither is it
won through good works. Good works are done through God's
grace in response to God's redemptive work in Christ. Accordingly,
Christ is the unique mediator between God and human beings. If
Roman Catholicism has recognized the intercession of the saints,
that is part of its understanding of the biblical injunction that we
must pray for one another, and the "we" includes not only believers
on earth, but those who have gone before us as saints in God's
presence in heaven. Such intercession is useful and salutary but in
no way necessary in the sense in which the mediation of Jesus
Christ is necessary. Any intercession on the part of the saints must
be accepted by God and joined to the supreme intercession of the
one high priest Jesus Christ. There is no other name by which we
may be saved, as Acts 4:12 affirms.

3. (**Jesus Christ, a Personal Savior** vs. salvation by belonging
to a church) While the Catholic Church proclaims the all-suffi-
ciency of the redemptive death and resurrection of Jesus Christ, it
acknowledges that Christians must respond in faith and commitment to Christ so that God's redemptive grace may transform them
as children of God. Therefore, encountering Christ and believing in
him in a personal way is very much part of Roman Catholic
thought. Jesus Christ redeemed a people—that is why we belong to

a church—and one becomes part of that people by adhesion to Christ. Baptism of infants, which makes them part of the Christian family of God, in no way is meant to substitute for the later personal decision that is intrinsically a Christian demand. In the wholeness of Christian life baptism and personal commitment must accompany each other.

4. **(The Sacrifice of Christ on the Cross, Once and for All** vs. Catholic masses as sacrifices offered by priests) Following the New Testament injunction of Jesus, "Do this in commemoration of me," the Catholic Church in her liturgy regularly breaks the bread which is the body of Christ and offers the cup which is the communion in his blood. It accepts fully the teaching of the Epistle to the Hebrews that the sacrifice of Jesus Christ on the cross is once and for all; there is no need for other sacrifices. The liturgy of the Last Supper which we call the mass is sacrifice in the sense that it makes present again for Christians of different times and places the possibility of participating in the body and blood of Christ in commemoration of him, proclaiming the death of the Lord until he comes. The mass is in no way a separate sacrifice from the sacrifice of the cross; it is not a new sacrifice replacing the sacrifice of the cross or adding to it as if that sacrifice were insufficient. Jesus, the Catholic Church holds, is the one high priest of the new covenant. If we Catholics refer to our clergy as priests, that terminology recognizes that when a Christian, designated by ordination, presides at the eucharist, which recalls the death of the Lord until he comes, that person represents Jesus the high priest and not merely the community. Our doctrine of the mass as re-presenting the one priestly sacrifice of Jesus is in our judgment fully biblical.

5. **(Christ as the Savior** vs. the church and its sacraments as salvific) Christ saves Christians in and through the church. The church, which is the body of Christ, for which he gave himself, has great dignity and importance, but does not save. We believe that Christ is operative in the sacraments of the church and that it is Christ who gives the grace that touches lives. The Catholic teaching that the sacraments work *ex opere operato* never should be understood to mean that the sacrament of itself, independently of Christ, is effective. That formula is meant to say that the efficacy of the sacraments is not dependent on the clergyperson or administrator

of the sacraments. Rather, for those who are disposed to receive his grace, Christ is operative in the sacraments.

6. (**Christ as Head of the Church** vs. the pope) Roman Catholics believe that Jesus Christ is the head of the body which is the church. No human can take his place, dispensing with his headship. The pope has no authority independent of Christ or in rivalry to him. Even as the New Testament speaks of overseers or bishops guiding individual churches, the pope is an overseer through whom Christ supplies guidance to the whole church, keeping it in the truth of the gospel.

7. (**All Human Beings Need Redemption** vs. the exaltation of Mary) In Catholic faith Mary, like all other descendants of Adam, had to be redeemed through Christ. We honor her especially for two biblical reasons: (a) She is the mother of Jesus who is Lord and God; (b) According to Luke 1:26–38 she is the first one to hear the good news of Jesus' identity and to say, "Be it done to me according to your word"—thus becoming the first disciple to meet Jesus' standard of hearing the word of God and doing it. We believe that God gave her special privileges, but these are related to the graces of discipleship given through Christ and in no way divinize her. All believers in Christ are delivered by his grace from the sin of Adam; all believers in Christ will be raised bodily from the dead. Catholics believe that Mary, the first one to profess belief in Christ as revealed by an angel, was through Christ's grace the first to be totally free from Adam's sin (conceived without sin) and the first to be raised bodily (assumed into heaven). While we acknowledge that these doctrines of the immaculate conception and assumption of Mary are not found in the New Testament, we hold them as consonant with the picture in Luke of Mary as the first one to believe, and with the picture in John where the mother of Jesus is especially honored as Jesus hangs on the cross.

8. (**The Second Coming of Christ** vs. human good works establishing the kingdom) We Catholics believe in the second coming of Christ. For us that means that God has yet to establish fully His kingdom and to judge the world. All this will be accomplished through Christ and is not attainable by human endeavor. As for when, through the coming of Christ, God will establish His kingdom, we believe in the teaching of Jesus recorded in Acts 1:7: "It is

not for you to know the times or seasons which the Father has fixed by His own authority." All human guesses as to the time of the second coming must yield to that biblical teaching.

9. (**Private Interpretation of Scripture** vs. church control) We Catholics do not exaggerate the principle that the church is the interpreter of Scripture. The Roman Catholic Church has rarely, if ever, defined what a text meant to the person who wrote it. The church encourages interpreters of Scripture to discover with all the scholarly means available to them what individual passages meant when they were written and encourages all its members to read the Bible for spiritual nourishment. Church interpretation for Catholics deals primarily, not with what the biblical text meant when it was written, but with what it means for the life of the Christian community in subsequent eras. On essential issues it maintains that the Spirit who inspired the Scriptures will not allow the whole community of believers to be misled about faith and moral behavior. Individuals from their Bible reading may come to radical conclusions; some have even denied the divinity of Christ, the resurrection, creation, and the Ten Commandments. The Catholic Church will take its guidance on such biblical matters from the long tradition of Christian teaching stemming from reflecting on the Bible.

10. (**Literal Inerrancy of the Bible** vs. inerrancy limited by salvific intent) The Roman Catholic Church teaches that the Bible communicates without error that truth which God intended for the sake of our salvation. Affirming biblical inerrancy in that sense, it also resists modern attempts to make the Bible answer problems that the biblical authors never thought of. It resists attempts to take biblical texts which envisioned other situations and apply them without qualification to situations of our times. Some of the conflicts between Roman Catholic practices and "literal" interpretations of the Bible rest precisely on this point. The Roman Catholic Church believes that none of its positions are in conflict with the literal interpretation of the Scriptures, when "literal" means what the author intended in his times as a communication of the truth that God wanted for the sake of our salvation. It resists the use of biblical interpretation to support scientific or historical statements that lay beyond the competency of the biblical authors in their times.

INDEX OF SUBJECTS TREATED IN THE QUESTIONS

(The numbers listed below *refer to Questions,* not to pages.)

BOOKS BY RAYMOND E. BROWN (1990)

Paulist Press
New Testament Essays
Priest and Bishop
The Virginal Conception and Bodily Resurrection of Jesus
Peter in the New Testament (editor)
Biblical Reflections on Crises Facing the Church
Mary in the New Testament (editor)
The Community of the Beloved Disciple
The Critical Meaning of the Bible
Antioch and Rome (with J. P. Meier)
The Churches the Apostles Left Behind
Biblical Exegesis and Church Doctrine
Responses to 101 Questions on the Bible

Doubleday
The Gospel According to John (2 vols., Anchor Bible Commentary)
The Birth of the Messiah
The Epistles of John (Anchor Bible Commentary)

Liturgical Press (Collegeville, Minn.)
The Gospel and Epistles of John—A Concise Commentary
The Book of Deuteronomy (OT Reading Guide)
A Coming Christ in Advent (Matthew 1 and Luke 1)
An Adult Christ at Christmas (Matthew 2 and Luke 2)
A Crucified Christ in Holy Week (Passion Narratives)

Prentice Hall
The New Jerome Biblical Commentary (editor)

Macmillan
Jesus God and Man (08400)

Michael Glazier (Wilmington, Del)
Recent Discoveries and the Biblical World

Many of the above have been published in England by Geoffrey Chapman

Other Books
in this series

101 QUESTIONS AND ANSWERS ON THE BIBLICAL TORAH
by Roland E. Murphy, O. Carm.

101 QUESTIONS AND ANSWERS ON THE CHURCH
by Richard P. McBrien

101 QUESTIONS AND ANSWERS ON CONFUCIANISM,
DAOISM, AND SHINTO
by John Renard

101 QUESTIONS AND ANSWERS ON PAUL
by Ronald D. Witherup, S.S.

101 QUESTIONS AND ANSWERS ON VATICAN II
by Maureen Sullivan, O.P.

Other Books
under the former series title

RESPONSES TO 101 QUESTIONS ON THE DEAD SEA SCROLLS
by Joseph A. Fitzmyer, S.J.

RESPONSES TO 101 QUESTIONS ABOUT JESUS
by Michael L. Cook, S.J.

RESPONSES TO 101 QUESTIONS ABOUT FEMINISM
by Denise Lardner Carmody

RESPONSES TO 101 QUESTIONS ON THE PSALMS
AND OTHER WRITINGS
by Roland E. Murphy, O. Carm.

RESPONSES TO 101 QUESTIONS ON DEATH AND
ETERNAL LIFE
by Peter C. Phan